D0615251

the
SERMON
on the
MOUNT

A Layman's Guide to Jesus' Most Famous Sermon

ROGER L. SHINN

festival
books

ABINGDON/*Nashville*

THE SERMON ON THE MOUNT

A Festival Book

Copyright 1954, 1962 United Church Press

All rights reserved
Festival edition published by Abingdon, May 1979
ISBN 0-687-37556-8

The scripture quotations in this publication are (unless
otherwise indicated) from the Revised Standard Version of
the Bible, copyrighted 1946 and 1952 by the Division of
Christian Education, National Council of Churches, and are
used by permission.

PRINTED IN THE UNITED STATES OF AMERICA

CONTENTS

1 : THE SERMON ON THE MOUNT TODAY

ANYONE approaching the Sermon on the Mount is wise to remember a saying from Mark Twain, who was more honest about his troubles than most of us are about ours. He had heard people complain that the Bible is hard to understand. But he said he was bothered more by the parts of the Bible that he *could* understand than by the parts he could *not* understand.

This statement fits the Sermon on the Mount. Occasionally, as we study it, we find ourselves bothered by the first problem. We do not understand, and we wish we might know with certainty exactly what Jesus meant. But more often the words are so clear that we can have no doubt about their meaning. Then the real trouble comes, because we know what a change they call for in our lives, and we hesitate to make that change. We feel uneasy when we face a description of ourselves as God would have us be.

Christ Speaks to Us

Throughout the centuries since these words were first recorded, people have responded in many ways to the Sermon on the Mount. Probably you have often heard two common opinions about it. The first opinion is all approval. We might expect that in the church. But curiously, skeptics outside the church will frequently say something like this: "I have my arguments with the churches and their beliefs, but when it comes to the religion of the Sermon on the Mount, I'm all for that."

The second opinion is negative. We find it often among doubters and non-Christians. Frequently it appears within the church. It uses words like these: "The Sermon on the Mount is a lot of beautiful idealism, but it isn't practical. It won't work in this kind of world."

It is strange that one document can provoke such completely contrary interpretations. Perhaps the reason is that few people are able to come to the Sermon on the Mount and to consider without prejudice what it says. Those who are able to do this, face both of Mark Twain's problems. First they must try honestly to understand it. Then they must come to terms with what they find.

For Christians the Bible is a living book through which the living God speaks to persons today. We cannot assign the Bible —especially we cannot assign Jesus—to some past century and let the matter rest there. Christ is addressing us as truly as he addressed his disciples in Palestine.

The purpose of this book is to interpret the meaning of the Sermon on the Mount for us today. There are other valid purposes for studying the Bible. Many books of magnificent scholarship examine historical and literary questions about the New Testament. We can understand Jesus' teachings more accurately because archaeologists and historians have probed into the past and other specialists have analyzed the biblical documents in their original languages. This book, though it often echoes the conclusions of such studies, has a different purpose. It concentrates on the question that all Christians must face: what does Jesus' teaching mean for our faith and living today?

Using the Bible

The Bible is more important than all the comments about the Bible. The most important part of getting at the Sermon on the Mount is to go directly to the Sermon on the Mount. It is short—shorter than the average Sunday morning sermon. Three and a half columns of a newspaper will hold it all. In the New Testament it is printed in chapters 5—7 of the Gospel according to Matthew.

Some of the same teachings of Jesus appear in Luke 6:20-49, in what has been called "The Sermon on the Plain." Also, many of the sayings in Matthew are found scattered through Luke in various settings.

These and other similar facts lead most biblical scholars to say that Matthew, who likes to organize his materials topically, gives us more than a single sermon. He and Luke started with the same core of materials—a set of teachings, mostly in poetry, which the disciples memorized as Jesus taught. To this core Matthew frequently added other related sayings of Jesus. Sometimes when a sentence in Matthew is not entirely clear, a look at the wording and the setting in Luke will bring out the meaning.

In this book each of the remaining chapters takes up a part of the Sermon on the Mount. Immediately following the chapter heading is the reference to Matthew. Look it up and read it carefully, because everything else in the chapter depends on it. The second reference is to the parallel passage in Luke. Sometimes this is very important; sometimes it adds nothing to what Matthew reports. Then comes a third reference that shows how other parts of the Bible take up the same theme.

For Further Study

If you can do more reading on the Sermon on the Mount, the following books will be helpful.

Archibald M. Hunter, *A Pattern for Life* (Westminster Press, 1953). This is a short and helpful book, entirely on the Sermon on the Mount.

The Interpreter's Bible, Volume VII (Abingdon Press, 1951), offers two helps. Amos N. Wilder's article, "The Sermon on the Mount," is a masterpiece. The commentary on Matthew 5—7, written by Sherman E. Johnson and George A. Buttrick, gives excellent guidance.

Martin Dibelius, *The Sermon on the Mount* (Scribner's, 1940). This is the work of a great German scholar of the New Testament. It is most helpful to readers who have some technical training in biblical studies.

2 : THE SPIRITUAL REVOLUTION

From the Sermon on the Mount read Matthew 5:1-3.
For the parallel passage see Luke 6:20, 24.
To follow up the theme look at Jeremiah 9:23-24; Matthew 18:1-4.

❧ THE FIRST sentence in the Sermon on the Mount strikes the revolutionary note characteristic of that revolutionary person—Jesus of Nazareth. We often miss this fact, because Jesus' words are so familiar. Like worn knives that have lost their cutting power, the sentences may lose their edge and even soothe rather than cut us. So try, as you study the Sermon on the Mount, to read with fresh imagination—as though you had never heard it before. You may be surprised at the result. Take the words seriously and they may anger you, annoy you, inspire you. They will hardly bore you. For they are revolutionary words.

Of course, Jesus was not trying to organize a revolt or seize the government. The traditional bearded bomb-thrower and the clever modern conspirator spit at his teaching. Jesus is more radical than the most radical of our political revolutionaries, but in a different way. He seeks a different kind of power. He has different goals.

Dr. Robert J. McCracken, pastor of New York's Riverside Church, tells how, in his teaching days, a college student enthusiastically urged him to read *The Communist Manifesto*. Although the teacher had read it before, he offered a bargain. He would read the Marxist *Manifesto* if the student would read the "Manifesto of Jesus." The student was startled to find, in that first sermon attributed to Jesus, these words:

> "The Spirit of the Lord is upon me,
> because he has anointed me to preach good news to the poor.
> He has sent me to proclaim release to the captives
> and recovering of sight to the blind,
> to set at liberty those who are oppressed,
> to proclaim the acceptable year of the Lord" (Luke 4:18-19).

No wonder the Christian gospel has caused "revolutions" wherever it has gone. The apostles were accused of turning the world upside down (Acts 17:6). They might have answered that they were trying to turn a topsy-turvy world right side up. For they sought no dictatorship, no kingly power. Their activities heralded the kingdom of God, which Jesus had proclaimed.

The Issue

A comparison will help us to catch the central idea of Jesus' revolution. In *Ruddigore*, a Gilbert and Sullivan opera, we get some advice which, though intended to be comic, most of us take rather seriously:

> If you wish in the world to advance
> Your merits you're bound to enhance,
> You must stir it and stump it,
> And blow your own trumpet,
> Or, trust me, you haven't a chance!

Compare that ditty with some other words, meant seriously but more likely to be taken as a joke. In 1918 Eugene V. Debs, the famous socialist, said:

. "While there is a lower class, I am in it; while there is a criminal element, I am of it; while there is a soul in prison, I am not free."

When we realize that Debs was anything but an orthodox Christian, we have to say with embarrassment that his words come closer to those of Jesus than do most of our own. They disturb us in the same way that the Sermon on the Mount does. For in our most generous moments we may wish that there were no lower classes, but we still prefer (so long as there are class differences) to find ourselves with the comfortable and secure.

But why do we disagree with Jesus? Do we misunderstand him? If so, do we deliberately misunderstand, or is it an accident? A look at just the first verse of the Sermon on the Mount may tell us. "Blessed are the poor in spirit, for theirs is the kingdom of heaven." Three terms in that one sentence are strange to us: kingdom of heaven, blessed, poor in spirit. If we understand them, we understand the sentence. And the one sentence gives us the clue to Jesus' whole message.

The Promise of God's Kingdom

Every week millions of people in this world mutter the phrase, "Thy kingdom come." If they really meant it, and knew what they meant, earthly kingdoms would tremble. They should know what it means, for it comes out of the Lord's Prayer and is the central theme in the Lord's teaching. Jesus began his public career with the proclamation, "Repent, for the kingdom of heaven is at hand" (Matt. 4:17). The sermon starts with the promise of this same kingdom of heaven (as Matthew calls it) or kingdom of God (Mark and Luke).

The kingdom of God is God's sovereignty over a community and a world that acknowledges him. It is God's answer to the evils of a world that rebels against him and tries to deny his lordship. It is not a kingdom which can be located on a map, but it is as real as any of the passing empires of history. We can understand it best by looking at it in three stages.

1. The kingdom of God has existed as long as the world, for God is the ruler of all he has created. An ancient Hebrew prayer begins: "Blessed art thou, O Lord our God, King of the world." But evil powers refuse to acknowledge God. They rebel against him. So, long before the time of Jesus, the Jewish people had begun to look for a Messiah and an act of God to conquer evil.

2. Jesus taught that this kingdom of God was "at hand," "drawing near," even "in your midst." God was acting to invade human history and defeat evil. Those who had eyes to see could already discern the signs of the times. Then—Christians believe —God did just what Jesus said he would do. But God did not do it in the way that people expected. He did it through the crucifixion of Jesus, through the resurrection, through the gift of the Holy Spirit. Faithful followers of Christ may now by faith and action enter into the life of God's kingdom.

3. God's activity is not finished. The world still goes its evil ways, often more ready to serve devilish causes than to serve God. Christians expect God to complete his work. Beyond this age is an inexhaustible future in which God will continue his work. His kingdom includes all of time and of eternal life.

So, it is sometimes said, Christians live "between the times." We live between earth and heaven, between God's act in Christ and the completion of that act. We see all the contrasts between the ways of the world and the ways of God, as described in the Sermon on the Mount. Yet right now we can serve him. We can enter into a sacred fellowship of God and men where the kingdom of God is a real power among us.

Thus when we read the Sermon on the Mount, we (like the first hearers) can respond to promises of a future divine kingdom. But more, we (better than those first hearers) can recognize that something of the power of this future kingdom is already ours if we respond to God's love, shown us in Christ.

That Mysterious Word—Blessed

The opening verses of the Sermon on the Mount are called "The Beatitudes." The word beatitude means blessedness, or the highest happiness. With a capital B it refers to the sayings of Jesus which start, "Blessed are. . . . "

But a word like blessedness calls for some thinking. Just what does it mean? It has a strange flavor to it, and we do not use it often. Our word happiness may come close, but it is often too trivial a word. Modern slang may even say, "He had a few drinks and was getting happy." We need to get beyond that word.

The word used in the New Testament is not the common Greek word for happiness. It refers to the attainment of an ideal and a goal. As soon as you read the Beatitudes, you realize that Jesus is talking about something far deeper than what most people mean by happiness.

Yet the word does not mean something mournfully pious and sanctimonious. It is a word of exclamation, of profound congratulation. It has been translated: "Hail you!"—"O the blessedness of!"—"How happy!" It has a fervor of joy and enthusiasm about it: "Blessed are you that weep now, for you shall laugh" (Luke 6:21). It is sometimes applied to God himself. And it is the expression of God's favor and God's mercy upon us. So, sometimes not realizing what we are doing, we "ask the blessing"—that is, ask God's blessing upon our families—at mealtime.

Who Shall Enter God's Kingdom?

Of all the ways we might think of to find happiness, Jesus picks the last. Slashing through our eager ambitions, our goals, our hopes, he promises the kingdom of God to the "poor in spirit." So Matthew reports it. The record in Luke is even more startling: "Blessed are you poor, for yours is the kingdom of

God. . . . But woe to you that are rich, for you have received your consolation" (Luke 6:20, 24).

These are strange words, easily misunderstood. Jesus is not pronouncing a blessing on all people who are "hard up"—however selfish or wicked they may be. Yet, though we may not like it, he uses words with economic significance. He reverses our ordinary scale of values. The motto of the newspaperman, Joseph Pulitzer, owes much to Jesus: "Comfort the afflicted and afflict the comfortable." Jesus consistently taught that possessing wealth is dangerously close to trusting in wealth and thereby rejecting the kingdom of God. (See Luke 12:16-21 and Matthew 19:16-26.)

The word was often used in Palestine to mean saintly. Especially in Jesus' time, under foreign rule, most of the rich people compromised with the pagan rulers and became worldly and irreligious, while the poor more often remained faithful. When Jesus blesses the poor, he means those who feel spiritual need, who make no claims for their own adequacy, who "do not have an inflated spirit" (Augustine), who are humble before God and yearn for his kingdom.

A foe of Christianity in the second century ridiculed this religion because it attracted "the very dregs of the population, peasants, mechanics, beggars, and slaves." One Christian, named Origen—though himself a distinguished scholar who might have refuted the charge by pointing to his own learning—answered that the church could take pleasure in following its Master by appealing to those whom others despised.

A Challenge

Now, after studying the three key terms, you can understand the first strange sentence of the Sermon on the Mount. Read it once more. Then ask: Does anybody believe it? Do you believe it? What shall we do about this embarrassing challenge of Jesus of Nazareth?

Sören Kierkegaard, the Danish philosopher and theologian, complained that modern churchmanship is only play-acting. We have no thought of seriously believing Jesus. We are like tourists who, solely for amusement, use a quaint and obsolete guidebook. While we travel comfortably by rail, we read the book's description of the perilous roads and trails. Smoking a cigar in a snug café, we read of dangerous robber bands who assault travelers in the region. Similarly, says Kierkegaard, while we enjoy our worldly comforts, we get a faint emotional glow from reading of the Jesus whom we would never be so foolish as to obey.

Perhaps Kierkegaard was right. "Blessed are the poor in spirit." Christians have to come to terms with Jesus on that.

3 : TURNING OUR VALUES UPSIDE DOWN

From the Sermon on the Mount read Matthew 5:4-9.
For the parallel passage see Luke 6:21, 25.
To follow up the theme look at Matthew 20:25-28.

THE POET Shelley, in his "Ozymandias," tells of a traveler who, in an ancient land, saw the ruins of a once great monument. In the midst of the desert stood "two vast and trunkless legs of stone." Half-buried in the nearby sand was the shattered, sneering face which had once been part of the statue. We are not told whether war or nature had destroyed the once impressive object. We learn only this:

And on the pedestal these words appear:
"My name is Ozymandias, king of kings:

> Look on my works, ye Mighty, and despair!"
> Nothing beside remains. Round the decay
> Of that colossal wreck, boundless and bare
> The lone and level sands stretch far away.

So time destroys the achievements of powerful men. Even their monuments become pathetic reminders of their feebleness.

A witty modern writer suggests that along with the engraving on the pedestal may also be found the scratched names of Mr. and Mrs. Dukes and various other tourists. Obviously Ozymandias did not awe them. History is hard on boasters. Every cemetery reminds us that

> The paths of glory lead but to the grave.

Yet still we love glory. And when Jesus tells us the paths that lead to blessedness, we cannot bring ourselves to believe him. For he turns our usual values upside down.

The Mourners, the Hungry, the Pure

Each Beatitude of Jesus tells how the kingdom of God reverses the obvious situation. Each statement makes us readjust our thinking.

Those who mourn shall be comforted. The aim is not to make a miserable, weeping world. Some misery comes out of self-centeredness, frustrated ambition, the bitter emptiness of those who cannot love. There is no comfort in such misery.

But in this world only the crude and insensitive can avoid sorrow. In Handel's *Messiah* we sing of Jesus (in the words from Isaiah) as "a man of sorrows and acquainted with grief." Sympathetic spirits will often know grief.

In desperate periods of history some men always respond by saying that we cannot afford to be sensitive. If today a person were to feel grief for all the pains of the world, he could not bear the load. Hence we steel ourselves, stifle emotion, avoid thinking about pain and suffering. The world was in turmoil in

Jesus' time too. The Stoic philosophers were saying: "Don't mourn. Self-control is the answer to sorrow." A few decades after Jesus, Epictetus—a great man in many respects—said: Love your wife and your children, but not so much that you will be hurt when they die.

But Jesus would have us enlarge and deepen our sympathies. For those who weep shall laugh (Luke); those who mourn shall be comforted. The word comfort has been cheapened. We have softened it to suit our love of being "comfortable." But look at the word. You can see it in the root of our word fortify. Those who are comforted find the peace that comes from strength. No wonder Christians find in Jesus the fulfillment of the great prophecy: "Comfort my people" (Isa. 40:1).

The hungry and thirsty shall be satisfied. Not all hungers can be satisfied. One may have a craving for wealth as long as one lives. Most often it is not satisfied. Who has all the wealth he thinks he needs? Or who, when he gets it, finds satisfaction? Like wealth, many of life's goals are either never attained or, when attained, turn out to be empty.

To hunger and thirst after righteousness is different. Today we have narrowed the word righteousness to refer to good conduct. To those who heard Jesus, it meant much more. It included justice, generosity, goodwill, compassion; it even came close to meaning salvation. For all this we may hunger and thirst.

Few Americans know what hunger is. If a meal is an hour late, we think we are hungry. Maybe we know thirst a bit better; everyone has felt a parched throat on a torrid day. But with water coolers and soft-drink machines in most buildings, it takes imagination to feel the craving of intense thirst. If we knew such thirst—for righteousness—we would be blessed in God's kingdom.

The pure in heart shall see God. Aristotle had taught that the man of genius and education, if he had all the advantages of

life, could contemplate God. For women, children, slaves, this
was impossible, as it was for the ignorant and poverty-stricken.
Jesus turns the whole system over. He has already blessed the
poor in spirit, for whom Aristotle could have only condescen-
sion. Now he gives the one qualification for seeing God—purity of heart.

The Hebrew, unlike many of the surrounding peoples, was
little interested in the mystical vision of God. He saw God in
God's activity, in divine judgment and mercy—and now, at
last, in Christ. Albert Schweitzer has written of Jesus: "He
commands. And to those who obey, be they wise or simple, he
will reveal himself through all that they are privileged to experience in his fellowship of peace and activity, of struggle and
suffering, till they come to know, as an inexpressible secret,
who he is. . . . "[1]

To obey Christ, says Schweitzer, is to know God through
Christ. But who obeys? The pure in heart. The best commentary
is the story of Nicodemus in John 3. Not intelligence, education, leadership, but rebirth into purity of heart is needed.

The Meek, the Merciful, and the Peacemakers

Now (rearranging the order slightly) come three blessings
that have been all but silenced by the thunder of our warlike
world.

The meek shall inherit the earth. People love to laugh at this
one. What an idea! All the earth that the meek inherit is six
feet in a cemetery plot! (But that's a bad example to prove the
point. In cemeteries the conquerors are like the rest of us.)

However, meek does not mean cowardly or soft. The tremendous Moses was called the meekest of men (Numbers 12:3).
Jesus was meek (Matthew 11:29)—heroically meek. There is
nothing of Casper Milquetoast in this Beatitude.

---

[1] *Out of My Life and Thought* by Albert Schweitzer, pp. 71-72. Holt,
Rinehart and Winston, Inc., 1933. Used by permission.

Benito Mussolini, when asked what his ambition was, replied: "I am obsessed by this wild desire—it consumes my whole being: I want to make a mark on my era with my will, like a lion with its claw! A mark like this. . . ." And, using his fingernail as a claw, Mussolini gouged a scratch in the back of a chair.

That is not meekness, but it is not strength either. Compare Abraham Lincoln, both stronger and meeker than Mussolini. As a young lawyer he had been crushed by the rude treatment of a distinguished colleague, Edwin Stanton. But, ignoring pride, he appointed to the cabinet this man who had snubbed him. And Stanton learned to work intimately with the president whom he had regarded as "the Illinois Ape." Similarly, when General McClellan's repeated insolence to the President made others furious, Lincoln refused to worry. "I will hold McClellan's horse," he said, "if he will only bring us success." No weak personality can be so meek.

But how shall the meek inherit the earth? Jesus' words echo Psalm 37:11. To inherit anything meant in the Hebrew tradition to receive it as a divine gift. (So Christians are "fellow heirs with Christ," as Paul says in Romans 8:17.) Jesus is not explaining how to acquire real estate, although even here we might ask how much the Mussolinis, with their disdain for meekness, accomplish. The real promise refers to the kingdom of God, where the meek are granted the divine blessing.

The merciful shall obtain mercy. Mercy represents one of the richest words in the Hebrew tradition. It is one of the key qualities of God. It is loving-kindness, generosity to the weak and helpless, continued love for people even when they have not been faithful. It is opposed to the rugged individualism in which men compete for gain by forcing the weak under.

The newspapers pointed out when Lavrenti Beria, former chief of the Russian secret police, was arrested and "liquidated," that this man was really the victim of his own methods. Locked in the prison where he had locked others, subjected to treatment that he had taught his secret police, tried in the sort of trial he had helped to engineer, he was mocked by his own cruelty. It would have been ironical if, in his cell, he had looked in a Bible and chanced to see the words, "Blessed are the merciful, for they shall obtain mercy."

The peacemakers shall be called sons of God. The Prince of Peace was the one Son of God. We, if we are peacemakers, can be called sons of God. We have been told, in this cruel century of history, that the only purpose of war is victory. But surely peace is the only purpose that can justify war. Even the warrior, if he is a Christian, will be less a warrior than a peacemaker.

Real peacemaking takes courage. It is not a matter of crying peace where there is no peace. It is not the avoidance of trouble in proud isolation. It is not indifference to the sufferings of others. Peace is a call to heroic activity. It is God's work, in which we may share.

The Perpetual Conflict

It is a long time since the human race first heard these words of the Beatitudes. But they still sound almost as strange as they ever did. Jesus stands in perpetual conflict with the ways of the world. Persuasive philosophies keep trying to undermine these "Blessings."

(a) Many today, like Plato and Aristotle before Christ, say that true understanding and happiness are reserved for the mentally brilliant. Brains, they say, will save us. The scholars and technicians, not the "poor in spirit" or the "pure in heart," will lead humanity out of its despair.

(b) Some find in economic power the key to success. Marxism sneers at religion as an "opiate" devised by the wealthy to keep the poor meek and content in their misery. American propaganda often says that our tremendous production and our high standard of living make us worthy to follow. Gradually we are realizing that such propaganda often makes other peoples despise rather than honor us.

(c) Various forms of ego-gratification promise happiness. Experts report that in primitive societies appeals to vanity sometimes succeed when all other motivations fail. Primitive man has been called "a peacock." We wonder whether civilized man is greatly different.

(d) Power and domination are powerful goals. Nietzsche, the German philosopher, scorned the "slave morality" of Christians and praised "master morality," the will to power. Laughing at sympathy and selflessness, he called them expressions of weakness.

To all these attitudes Christian faith makes a double reply. *First*, it reverses their valuations. Again and again it takes the side of the lowly. *Second*, it asserts that seeming weakness in reality may be strength. Mussolini and Nietzsche think that men cooperate, sympathize, and accept scorn or ridicule only because they are too weak to assert themselves. Christian faith replies that Mussolini and Nietzsche were the real pathological weaklings, that when a man has genuine strength he does not need to parade his power. So the Jewish scholar, Claude Montefiore, acknowledges in Jesus' message "an ethical teaching for heroes."

Missing the Point

Sometimes, instead of rejecting Jesus' teaching, we accept it too easily. We approve it because we do not even see the conflict with our usual ways. Thus visitors to the White House heard one President of the United States—never mind which one—say the following:

"The Sermon on the Mount is what we try to live by. If we can get all the world in that frame of mind, we will come nearer to stopping these terrible wars than by any other method I know of.

"We have become the leaders of the moral forces of the

world, leaders who believe that the Sermon on the Mount means what it says, leaders who believe that the law is a God-given law under which we live, that all of our traditions have come from Moses at Sinai and Jesus on the Mount. We are endeavoring to live and act by that law.

"The Russian Communists do not believe in a moral code and even go so far as to say there is no Supreme Being."

Some American churchmen approved those words for their "spirituality." But *The Christian Century*, one of the foremost Protestant magazines, said: "We wonder a little how recently he [the President] has read those three austere and humbling chapters from the Gospel according to Matthew."[2]

4 : THE COST OF DISCIPLESHIP

From the Sermon on the Mount read Matthew 5:10-12.
For the parallel passages see Luke 6:22-23, 26.
To follow up the theme look at 1 Peter 4:12-19; Romans 8:35-39; Revelation 3:14-22.

⚜ IN A STROKE of accurate wit Dean Inge of St. Paul's Cathedral in London once described the common longing for comfortable religion. He referred to a stanza of Reginald Heber's hymn, "The Son of God Goes Forth to War"—a stanza inspired by past Christian heroes:

> They climbed the steep ascent of heaven
> Through peril, toil, and pain:
> O God, to us may grace be given
> To follow in their train.

---

[2] *The Christian Century*, June 28, 1950, p. 782.

Many, said Dean Inge, prefer an easier way to heaven and would like to revise the last line of the verse to sing:

> To travel by the train.

Halford Luccock, in a comment on Dean Inge's verse, quotes the gushing woman who said: "We have the most up-to-date church in the country. We have inner springs in the pew cushions."

To all this a Christian might say: Welcome to comfortable Pullman cars and pew cushions *if* they remove some inconveniences and thus enable us to use our powers to conquer real difficulties. But God help us *if* we think that Christ offers us a path of comfort.

Suffering for Christ's Sake

Most of the Beatitudes are single, short sentences. They are cogently stated—originally in poetry—and could scarcely lose a word without losing the meaning. But when it comes to the blessing on the persecuted, Matthew records three sentences, each longer than any of the preceding Beatitudes. All this is no accident.

Recently biblical studies have shown us much about how our New Testament came to us. Obviously we do not have everything that Jesus ever said. If we take all the sayings of Jesus in the Bible (eliminating duplications in the different Gospels), we have a small quantity. A talkative person says more words in one single day.

What we have are those sayings which struck men so forcibly that they could not be forgotten. They spoke to burning needs. So Christians memorized them and passed them on, used them in sermons and letters and conversations, preserved them through the transition from the Aramaic to the Greek language until the days when they collected them into our Gospels.

Christians, facing death for their faith, treasured the sayings of their Lord about persecutions and sought to pass on his promises without losing a word. Here was a source of strength. Christ, their risen Lord, had also known persecution. His words and spirit were a living power. With Paul these Christians gloried that—whether in persecution, famine, or violent death— they were "more than conquerors through him who loved" them (Romans 8:35-37).

We sometimes hear a parent say: "I want my child brought up in a Christian atmosphere, so that he will stay out of trouble." There is a grain of truth in that idea. Christian character does overcome or bypass some troubles in life.

But can you imagine a parent bringing a child to Jesus with the words: "I want my boy to go with you, because you will keep him out of trouble"? How might Jesus reply? Perhaps he would say: "What are you talking about? Foxes have their holes, but I have no place to lay my head. This is no way to avoid trouble." (See Luke 9:57-58.) Or he might say: "Trouble is one thing I can guarantee. If your boy comes with me, he'd better prepare for self-denial, persecution—yes, cruel death." (See Matthew 16:24 and Mark 13:9-13.)

Once again Jesus upsets our ways of thought. Often in the Old Testament, and often today, people think of prosperity and esteem as a reward for goodness. With deep irony Kierkegaard says of a bishop of Denmark: "Without doubt, he would not hesitate to die for Christ, in the case of necessity, but he takes care that the case of necessity does not occur." And don't we all?

But Jesus' advice is the opposite. Not only does he bid us bear up under suffering. In bold and striking language he says: "Rejoice . . . and leap for joy!" (Luke 6:23) So, following Jesus, Paul wrote: "We rejoice in our sufferings" (Rom. 5:3). But why?

One reason that Jesus gives is that men persecuted the prophets of old and spoke well of the false prophets. We might think that a poor reason. Factually, of course, it is true. The stories of Amos and Jeremiah tell us how the prophet must often speak unpleasant words, while the false prophet yields to social pressure, salves guilty consciences, and adjusts his message to make people feel good. Naturally, men speak well of him.

What Jesus Promises

Hence we should rather—so Jesus thinks—accept persecution with the prophets than enjoy human approval with the false prophets. This logic may be unconvincing. But it may—if we are touched by Christ's spirit—command agreement. It promises us a place in what a great liturgical prayer calls "the glorious company of the apostles, the goodly fellowship of the prophets, the noble army of martyrs." This, says Christian faith, is reason to rejoice. But there is more to the promise. Jesus offers "the kingdom of heaven" and a great "reward" in heaven. What does he mean?

We can easily misunderstand this promise of reward. We may take it as an offer of a bargain: Be good now and you'll get paid off later. Accept poverty and suffering here, and you will be given "pie in the sky by-and-by." But Jesus often warns men that they cannot bargain with God. He tells us that the best of actions, when done with impure motives, are worthless. (We will see more of this in chapter 6.) There is no room here for selfishly playing the game for the highest stakes—giving up a payoff now for a bigger one later. Jesus does not say: "Blessed are you who accept persecution for the sake of future reward." No, he talks of persecution for righteousness' sake or for his sake. Rudolf Bultmann, one of the foremost New Testament scholars, says: "He promises reward precisely to those who obey not for the sake of reward."[1]

In Alan Paton's magnificent novel *Cry, the Beloved Country*, one of the natives of South Africa, a simple man with work-calloused hands, a member of a persecuted people, says this: "I have never thought that a Christian would be free of suffer-

---

[1] *Theology of the New Testament* by Rudolf Bultmann, Vol. I, p. 14. Charles Scribner's Sons, 1951. Used by permission.

ing. . . . For our Lord suffered. And I came to believe that he suffered, not to save us from suffering, but to teach us how to bear suffering. For he knew there is no life without suffering."[2]

So the reward is the sharing in the life and love of Christ.

This reward is not something for the future alone. It comes in "the kingdom of heaven," which, we remember, has come among us in Christ, although we wait for God to complete it. For the apostle Paul, the love of God in Christ is already so tremendous an experience that he is sure "neither death, nor life" can separate him from it (Romans 8:38-39).

Our Situation Today

Of course, all this can be very remote—something for ancient times only. We cannot go back to live in Palestine or the Roman Empire. Does Jesus really have anything to say to us today?

The answer is that the promise of Jesus has spoken as clearly to men in our time as it ever spoke in the past. The testimonies come from countless sources. From missionaries in foreign lands, from Christians scorned by their own kinsmen in non-Christian areas, from loyal churchmen persecuted by totalitarian governments come declarations of Christ's blessing and Christ's love.

Consider just one situation. We all know of the bitter persecution by Soviet rulers of the East German Church in 1952-53. Faithful pastors disappeared into the night. Young people met ridicule and exclusion in the schools because they acknowledged membership in the *Junge Gemeinde* (the youth fellowship) of the church. Laymen lost jobs and brought suffering upon their families because they confessed church membership. Yet out of that situation came testimonies of God's love that cannot be matched in America. Here are a few of the many responses:

1. A Christian, even while admitting his perplexities, said: "Perhaps God wants to bring suffering to hundreds and thou-

---

[2] *Cry, the Beloved Country* by Alan Paton, p. 227. Charles Scribner's Sons, 1948. Used by permission.

sands of Christians, because he wants them." Another, feeling that in the suffering God had *found* persons, spoke of "God's beloved East Zone."

2. In the persecution a Christian wrote: "Hate and fear have been vanquished by him who loved us. He himself is the peace, who has given us true and lasting peace with God and with our enemies."

3. A woman whose husband had been arrested said this: "Yes, the great joy and happiness which come from the freedom of the heart, they were the chief characteristics of my dear husband. And *this* joy cannot and will not be destroyed by any external calamity. This is my confident hope. For it is striking that this joy comes out only the more brightly in misery and darkness. Truly, God does not demand any sacrifice from us which he is not willing to bless a hundredfold in our hearts."

Coming Closer to Home

What does this all mean for us in our comfortable, casual American churches? Is there any blessing of Christ here?

One false answer we can quickly get out of the way: We are not serving Christ if we simply seek to generate hostilities against ourselves. Such is not persecution for Christ's sake. Perhaps this warning is not necessary. But we all know what is meant by a martyr-complex, and probably we all feel this temptation in minor ways. We can make ourselves miserable, simply out of egoism. Paul knew that one might even give his body to be burned—without love (1 Corinthians 13:3).

But when all this is said, we must recognize that Christ expected his followers to be persecuted. Why are we not being persecuted? Is it because the world has chosen to follow Christ instead of persecuting him? Surely the spirit of Christ through the centuries has made some difference. But there is a more cogent, perhaps a more honest reason. Even in New Testament times, some churches avoided the troubles that others were meeting. Are we like the church of Laodicea (Revelation 3:14-

22)—so lukewarm that we offend no one, except our Lord? Do men "speak well of" us because we are soft?

There is persecution in America. In the 1960's citizens and churchmen, believing that God's love includes persons of all races, have been battered and jailed. Men have endured bitter public ridicule because they believed in civil liberties for others.

There are other forms of persecution, too. A man loses a promotion because he refuses to play the game in cheap ways. A politician loses an election rather than lie to the voters. A pastor loses the call to a distinguished church instead of becoming a flatterer. In school, in business, in society at large someone earns scorn because he refuses to take the easy way.

If these things happen to us, not because of stubborn egoism or a self-righteous complex, but because of our love of God, Jesus tells us to rejoice. For then we are blessed of God.

5 : LIGHT AND SECRECY

From the Sermon on the Mount read Matthew 5:13-16; 6:1-18.

For the parallel passages see Luke 14:34-35; 11:33-36; 11:1-4.

To follow up the theme look at Matthew 23:1-12; Luke 18:9-14.

HEADS AND TAILS on a dime look different, but both are part of the same coin. Sometimes the truth, like the coin, shows two different faces. Frequently that is true of Jesus' sayings. His thoughts move with a vigor and penetration that strain the limits of language. His vocabulary is vigorous and exuberant, full of imaginative appeals. Often he meets a situation with a story instead of an explanation. Often instead of a simple statement he gives us a paradox.

Thus it is when Jesus tells his followers how they are related to the social world around them. To understand him we must pull together parts of two chapters in the Sermon on the Mount, because each side of the paradox helps explain the other. Christians are to *let their light shine* before men. Yet they are to do their good works *in secret*. If we take to heart either of these directions without the other, we can destroy the message of Jesus. How do the two faces of the coin go together?

We will not understand Jesus if we approach him as a lawmaker, prescribing rules for every situation in life. Rather, he uses specific situations to convey to us the *spirit* of the kingdom of God—a spirit that enters into everything we do. So let us look at each side of this paradox of Jesus in order to discover what it has to say about our inner attitudes and motives.

Salt and Light

"You are the salt of the earth." Here is a curious figure of speech. Human beings are not much like salt. But the striking metaphor has its purpose. A pinch of salt can flavor a whole meal. Salt is a preservative, often used in past times to save food from decay. So a few faithful disciples can affect society—giving zest to and saving from corruption a much larger group. But what about salt that is not salty? (Of course, there is no such thing; Jesus is simply continuing his figure of speech, which is meant to be bizarre enough to shake us out of our ruts.) It is useless. So is a disciple who has lost his enthusiasm and loyalty.

"You are the light of the world." Here is a more familiar figure of speech, common in the Jewish tradition. God has called his servant to be "a light to the nations" (Isa. 42:6). The rabbis sometimes thought of Israel as the light of the world. To this day candles are lighted on the altars of many a church during worship hours. A later New Testament book describes Christ as the light from God which shines into the darkness of the world (John 1:4-5).

Yet it must have sounded fantastic to suggest that this tiny band of weak disciples in an obscure land could be the light of the world. They were not even known in Rome, the headquarters of the world. Nevertheless, Jesus said that his followers, not the Caesars, were the light of the world. Now, centuries hence, we know well the feebleness of the Caesars and the light-giving power of that little group that followed Jesus. But to them these words of his must have seemed impossible—as impossible as much of the rest of the Sermon on the Mount.

Jesus bade these men—as he bids us—to let this light shine. It is senseless, yes criminal, to conceal a light that can bless the world. Let the beams stream afar!

Then the world will see us, recognize us, appreciate us—we think. But that is not what Jesus says. He tells us to fear men's glory, not to seek it. (Remember chapter 4.) But we may hope that our light will lead men to glorify, not us, but God.

So it is said that in the heart of Africa a man relieved of pain by the surgical skill of a foreigner looked up to ask, "But why have you come here to help us?" And he got the simple answer from Albert Schweitzer, "The Lord Jesus sent me."

Thus Jesus' words come true. But too seldom. Why is there so little sacred light in this shadowed world? When a few disciples have spread such magnificent illumination, why do millions give so little light?

Between 1940 and 1950 for the first time in history church members came to be a majority of the population. In the century 1850-1950, membership moved from a rather small minority to a substantial majority. But what difference has it made? We can hardly claim any startling change in our society. Has the salt lost its savor? Is it fit only to be "thrown out"?

When the French Communists once wanted to strengthen the party, instead of campaigning for more members they pared down the rolls. They knew that a few zealously loyal people, working out from their little cells, could shake a nation. Maybe they had learned that from Christians, who once understood it well but now usually forget it.

Serving in Secrecy

Now we turn the coin over and find Jesus telling us, not to let our good works be seen, but to do good in secret. The contradiction seems great; but it is resolved when we get at the basic concern of Jesus—our motives.

For, says Jesus, the purpose of our good works is to glorify God, to serve him, to express our love for God and our fellowmen. If this is honestly our purpose, we are not worried about getting credit for what we do. But too often our purpose is not genuine. Then we demand recognition. So our willingness to do our good works in secret becomes a real test of our sincerity.

Look at an example from a growing congregation which needed a new building. (The same thing may have happened often, but the recorded facts come from a single specific case.) The pastor and officers of the church, in planning the financial campaign, decided that contributions would be kept secret. The purpose was to make giving a genuine act of Christian devotion. As the campaign got under way, returns were disappointing. Some families were clearly doing their share; others, sometimes the wealthiest, were dragging their feet. So the officers reconsidered and decided to publicize contributions. Many contributors revised their pledges and the campaign succeeded. Some of the church members, who understood the Sermon on the Mount, were grateful for the new building, but disturbed by what they had learned about the motives for giving.

The same psychology works in still subtler ways. Charles Lamb wrote: "The greatest pleasure I know is to do a good action by stealth and have it found out by accident."

That statement shows up some of the devious traits of personality. We enjoy getting credit for doing good. But then, knowing Jesus' teaching, we obey him and do good secretly. Since we still like praise for our good deeds, we praise ourselves—both for doing good and for doing it secretly.

Then, if someone accidentally discovers our good deed, we can be triply proud. We have done the good, we have done it secretly, and we received the public credit! Sometimes we even pretend to be disappointed that the discovery has been made, when inwardly we are greatly pleased that our good deeds are known. Or—doesn't this really happen?—even while we do the good deed secretly, we hope (without quite admitting it to ourselves) that someone will discover it. Maybe we even "accidentally" leave a clue.

Appropriately enough, the Scriptures use the ugly word hypocrite here. This Greek word originally meant, in a quite harmless sense, an actor on the stage. The New Testament adapted the word to refer to the kind of acting we do in daily life—pretending to be generous when really we are merely looking for recognition, or pretending to be humble when really we are vain.

Jesus mentions three areas of action where we need to avoid this play-acting: good deeds, prayer, and fasting. In the case of good deeds, Jesus uses his typically vivid, exuberant language. The humorous words convey a serious meaning. Literally, we cannot prevent the left hand from knowing what the right hand does. Literally, the Palestinians did not blow trumpets to call attention to their almsgiving. But we easily get the meaning. (We still say, "If you don't blow your own trumpet, no one will blow it for you.")

Prayer is an especially significant problem. Here, of all places, sincerity should be complete. But many prayers are simply "empty phrases." (The Lord's Prayer, which Jesus gives at this point, will be the subject of chapter 8.)

Fasting represents the sacrifices we make because of our faith. We love to let others know that we are making a sacrifice—that we are giving up something to do a job for the church. But Jesus says: "No. Make your sacrifice joyfully and unobtrusively. God will reward you."

Summing It Up

Our everyday language recognizes at least in part what Jesus is getting at. "Don't be afraid to take a stand." "Don't blow your own horn." Here are two sayings that point in different directions. One suggests bold, public activity; the other suggests quiet modesty.

Yet we see immediately that the two do not necessarily disagree. Each has its place. The same person might consistently use both sayings. For both are getting at the motives that prompt our acts. When fear of popular disapproval or lethargy leads us to drift with the crowd, we need to think of the first. When pride tempts us to make some display, we need the second.

In a more profound way Jesus is telling us to live our lives before God. Sometimes this will mean that we let our light shine before men—doing good, confessing our faith—even though men may seek to embarrass us with their sneers. Sometimes it will mean that we serve God in secret, even though publicity might please us. Always it will mean the kind of sincerity that removes self-consciousness from our religious acts.

Of course, this is the most difficult of all tests because it concerns inmost motivations. Effort and will power can accomplish a lot, but they cannot in themselves change our motives or bring us to be less concerned with ourselves. Self-consciousness is a mountain that no quantity of determination can move. But it is one of those mountains which faith, and faith alone, can cast into the sea.

6 : THE OLD AND THE NEW

From the Sermon on the Mount read Matthew 5:17-37.
For the parallel passage see Luke 16:16-18.
To follow up the theme look at Jeremiah 31:31-34; Ezekiel 36:22-36.

NOTHING SEEMS MUCH OLDER than the pancakes that were fresh yesterday. The new dress or hat, the new car, the new toy for the children—all turn old in a few weeks or, at least, a few years. Collectors often specialize in old things, for they will keep getting older; nothing new will get any newer.

Yet human life craves the new. The old gets tiresome; we need renewal, freshening, invigorating. Fortunately, some things are perpetually new. The mysteries of love and hope, of sympathy and joy, are inexhaustible. However long we live with them, they are able to open up new worlds for us, to lead us into undiscovered riches of living.

The Christian faith has its source in the conviction of a new covenant—the phrase is often translated New Testament—which God offers mankind. It is the Christian faith that this covenant never grows old or dim or tarnished, because it is a living covenant. It is our belief that when we get bored with all of civilization's hectic attempts to find "something new and different," this age-old covenant remains fresh. Let us see why.

The Story of the Covenants

Jesus was talking to a group of people who were confident that they lived in a covenant-relationship with God. In the ancient days at Mount Sinai, God had said to Moses: "I have made a covenant with you and with Israel" (Exod. 34:27). The words of the covenant were preserved in the Ten Commandments. Through the centuries, when the Israelites sinned, the prophets called on the people to be faithful to their covenant. Everyone who heard Jesus knew of that covenant.

Many who heard him remembered also that the great prophet Jeremiah had foretold the days of a new covenant—written, this time, not on tablets of stone but upon the hearts of the people. This was to be a covenant of divine forgiveness. (See Jeremiah 31:31-34.)

Now, in a land already stirred by the fiery John the Baptist, Jesus appeared. Boldly he confronted the sacred tradition and said repeatedly: "You have heard that it was said . . . but I say. . . ." This rash effrontery was more than some conscientiously religious men could stand; their whole sense of what was sacred made them enemies of this bold impostor—as he seemed to them. But others recognized in him God's ambassador, bringing the promised new covenant.

Thus the Christian church has seen it through the ages. At the service of Holy Communion we read again the words of institution, "This is my blood of the covenant" (Matt. 26:28). The Christian faith is that in Christ the hope of the centuries was realized: the new covenant was established.

But the Lord of the new covenant did not deride the old covenant. Some Christians in the early centuries of the church did. They wanted to do away with the Old Testament, and reject the God of the Jews. The church, however, declared their views heretical—for Jesus had said that he came not to abolish the Law and the Prophets but to fulfill them. Notice the strong wording of Matthew 5:17-20, especially verse 18. Iota refers to the smallest letter in the Hebrew alphabet. The dot is an ornamental mark that the scribes used in writing. Although we know that Jesus was less concerned with minute details of the Law than with man's basic relation to God, he is here saying: If you truly understand what God asks in the Law, you will see that none of it (not an iota or dot) is lost in my teaching.

Yet Jesus' method was not to elaborate, develop, and bring up to date the Law by applying it to the many details of first-century Palestinian life. That was the method of the conscientious Pharisees. Jesus rather went to the heart of the Law, extracted its divinely-given meaning from the surrounding web of words and customs, and proclaimed the will of God in its purity. But to those who concentrated on the externals, Jesus appeared to be wrecking the most sacred of religious institutions.

What Is New in Jesus' Teaching?

Sometimes Jesus startled his listeners with a statement so new that they were shocked by it. More often his ideas were not new,

THE OLD AND THE NEW : 35

at least not in the sense that no one had ever thought of them before. Most of the sentences in the Sermon on the Mount have their parallels in the Old Testament or in the rabbinic writings of Jesus' time.

Sometimes we say that the newness of Jesus lies in his personality—in his powerful character which inspired men to faithful loyalty, in the vigor that shook them out of their ruts, in the holiness before which they felt ashamed, in the mercy that brought love into the lives of sinners. Sometimes we find his newness in the penetrating discrimination by which he evaluates old teachings, knows which to accept and which to reject, puts first things first, and subordinates what is secondary.

These ideas are true enough, but they do not quite get to the core of the matter. For Jesus' emphasis was not on his own personality or on a new and better law. His central message— as we have seen—was the gospel of the kingdom of God. It is this kingdom, which fulfills the best in the Law, which takes men's deepest yearnings and makes them deeper yet before it satisfies them. So the newness of Jesus is the power of the kingdom of God to make us new. We understand his sayings when we grasp them as expressions of that power.

So one of our foremost New Testament scholars writes:

"God demands more than that man should perform some particular commandments; he demands that man become a new being, living under the eyes of God and in the consciousness of his will. . . . For Christ has brought with him not the revelation of a new law but the message of the kingdom. Its purpose is to transform men, and a transformed humanity will be able to do more than men did under the government of the old Law. Man will recognize the will of God in every situation, even if the commandments of the Bible do not cover this situation."[1]

When we understand this we can see why the message of

---

[1] *The Sermon on the Mount* by Martin Dibelius, pp. 77-78. Charles Scribner's Sons, 1940. Used by permission.

Christ is as new in the twentieth century as it was in the first, and why it fulfills the highest ethics of our world as truly and as radically as it fulfills the ancient Jewish Law.

The Inwardness of Jesus' Ethic

Today we, like some of the Pharisees, are likely to find the causes of our troubles in the externals of life. Propagandists tell us that we can solve our problems by buying a new product, by getting (or getting rid of) a "new deal" in government, by new techniques of industry or of psychology. As T. S. Eliot says:

They constantly try to escape
From the darkness outside and within
By dreaming of systems so perfect that no one will need
    to be good.[2]

Of course, the Christian faith does not discourage our attempts to deal with the externals of life. But it tells us that no externals will take the place of Christ's message to the inmost self. His message, in one example after another, moves from the law governing actions to the inner motive.

(1) *From murder to hatred* (see Matthew 5:21-26). Laws can prescribe punishment for murder. But no government can outlaw anger and animosity. Only the kingdom of God can do that. For Jesus the seething resentment is as bad as the act that grows out of it. Jesus does not, of course, condemn honest and deeply-felt opposition to wrong. He is talking of the kind of anger that is an expression of envy or jealously and that takes satisfaction in the bad fortunes of another. Modern psychological discoveries throw an interesting light on the Christian teaching here, as they show how repressed hostilities can create in us a hell on earth. The answer obviously is not in allowing all hostilities to

---

[2] From "The Rock," reprinted from *Collected Poems 1909-1935* by T. S. Eliot. Harcourt, Brace & World, Inc., 1936. Used by permission.

erupt—not in letting anger become murder. What we need is inner healing. So Jesus "fulfills" one of the Ten Commandments —one article of the Old Covenant.

Verses 25-26 here present some problems of detail. Luke puts these verses in a different context (12:57-59). In Matthew they might be merely prudential advice. Actually they are a parable about man's relation to God. Every man is approaching God's judgment seat. We had better approach in humility and repentance, seeking God's mercy.

(2) *From adultery to lust* (see Matthew 5:27-32). Again Jesus moves from the overt act which a court of law might pass judgment on, to the inner disposition. If a man covets his neighbor's wife (in the words of the Ten Commandments), he "has already committed adultery with her in his heart." Once more recent psychology, showing the disastrous effects of repression, bears out what Jesus is saying; and once more the answer is not the discarding of all restraints upon conduct, but an inner transformation—a "fulfillment" of the Law.

Verses 29-30 show the seriousness of sin. Some religions actually endorse self-mutilation, and in rare cases Christians have taken these verses literally. However there is no evidence that those who knew Jesus ever understood him in this way. The complete paragraph makes the point clear. If inward lust is the problem, literal loss of a hand or eye will do no good. Jesus means, seriously, that an unhealthy personality is worse than loss of limbs.

NOTE: We cannot here make a study of Jesus' whole teaching on the family, though that would be richly rewarding. We should notice two things in passing. First, Jesus is not condemning sexual desire or sexual union as such. Jesus' teaching on marriage (see Mark 10:6-9) places the highest value on marital union. Second, his teaching on divorce allows no room for self-righteous criticism of divorced persons. Jesus teaches the sanctity and permanence of marriage so as to bring under judgment all the frivolity of our culture. But those who use his words (verse 32) to condemn others find his words (verse 28) convicting themselves of the same guilt.

(3) *From perjury to dishonesty* (see Matthew 5:33-37). American law does not convict a man of simple dishonesty—or who would be out of prison? It defines the crime of perjury, in which one tells a falsehood under the technical conditions of a prescribed oath. So it was with Jewish law. Detailed prescriptions marked the difference between oaths that were binding and those that were not (Matthew 23:16-22). Jesus swept aside all this. For a man of integrity a simple "yes" is adequate—better than the most complicated oath of a hypocrite. Some Christian groups to this day take Jesus literally and refuse to take oaths, but most Christians think he was emphasizing the need for a genuine trustworthiness that will make unnecessary all the intricate legal guarantees.

A Covenant of Grace

In all this we see Jesus' insistence, "Unless your righteousness exceeds that of the scribes and Pharisees, you will never enter the kingdom of heaven" (Matt. 5:20). The Pharisees were the models of conscientiousness. Aiming to be faithful to God and his covenant, they guarded themselves against many temptations by carefully seeking to live up to the Law. Jesus demands so much less—and yet so much more. The meticulous attention to detail can go by the way, if only the essential thing is present, the fulfillment of the Law in the spirit of the kingdom of God.

Augustine understood this when in the fifth century a convert asked him for a listing of his ethical obligations as a Christian. Augustine's answer cut to the heart of the problem in a short sentence: "Love—and do as you please." The one word includes everything. For if we truly love, what we please will please God.

The answer is simple, but not easy. For, as we study the Sermon on the Mount, we realize that there is no human love of such purity as to meet God's demand. We try all sorts of ways to soften these words of Jesus.

For example, when Jesus says, "every one who is angry with his brother shall be liable to judgment," we say that is asking too much. How can we make it easier? In ancient times someone slipped into the sentence an extra two words, *without cause.* Some of our manuscripts of the New Testament include that insertion. Whoever got that idea reasoned thus: to be angry without cause is the sin; anger with just cause is all right. But that is a dodge. We are never angry without what we can pretend is a cause. But Jesus asks for complete love. He makes no concessions to our weakness.

We are driven to ask, as the disciples did on a different occasion, "Then who can be saved?" The answer to us, as to them, is: "With men it is impossible, but not with God; for all things are possible with God" (Mark 10:26-27). We are saved by God's mercy, not by our goodness. Christianity is a gospel, not a law. The new covenant is a covenant of grace.

7 : LOVE FOR ENEMIES

From the Sermon on the Mount read Matthew 5:38-48.
For the parallel passage see Luke 6:27-36.
To follow up the theme look at Leviticus 19:1-2, 17-18; Romans 12:14-21; 1 Peter 2:18-25; 3:8-9.

THE MOST CONTROVERSIAL character in all history is Jesus of Nazareth. Now we come to some of his most controversial teachings—love for enemies, forgiveness for any wrong, returning good for evil. Many of the world's leaders have wiped their feet in disdain on these sayings. Others have been transformed by them.

Let us start by looking at these sayings in their original setting. We can get some help from Sholem Asch, a reverent Jew who takes Jesus more seriously than many Christians do. In his novel, *The Nazarene*, he shows us how Jesus might have seemed to those who saw him in the flesh. As he reconstructs the scene of the Sermon on the Mount, we watch the attitudes of the people around Jesus. The common people are listening in eager approval. The scribes and scholars stand apart, in intent concentration. As Jesus echoes their orthodox teachings, they nod in vigorous agreement. When he uses the daring words, "But I say unto you," their frowns and gestures show their outrage.

Then comes the point at which Jesus asks them to love their enemies and pray for their persecutors. As Sholem Asch describes it, ". . . when he said this, they stretched out their hands to each other in bewilderment and despair, as if they had to go forth the very next day and fulfill the commandment. They exchanged frightened glances, and said in utter confusion: 'Surely it were well if it could be so! But who can carry this out? An angel, not a man of flesh and blood!' "[1]

Standing at the edge of the crowd are two officers of the Roman army, their armor covered by civilian togas. They too are curious and amazed. Days afterwards one of them, worrying about what Jesus teaches, thinks this:

"He seeks to undo and wipe out everything that man has accumulated by experience, whatever has been won in the struggle for mastery and supremacy, everything that tradition has ratified, whatever custom and law have validated, everything that has been cultivated and is controlled by institutions, rulers and spiritual leaders—and to create in their place a new world and a new order founded on diametrically opposed principles. The things that we regard as virtues, as the highest achievements of man's peculiar and separate greatness, he would condemn as vices and defects; and contrariwise, vices and defects are exalted

---

[1] *The Nazarene* by Sholem Asch, p. 168. G. P. Putnam's Sons, 1939. Used by permission.

by him into high moral commandments. . . . To avoid anger and hatred, which are the parents of battle and victory, to renounce, to love your foe, to fly from the battlefield before you have set foot on it, to forgive your enemies their sins in order that your father in heaven may forgive you yours. . . .

"I saw in this man the epitome of all dangers. . . . He was a more desperate enemy than Carthage had been of old, or any other hostile state since then."[2]

We have to ask ourselves, could it be that this Roman officer understood Jesus better than our churches do today? Quite possibly he did.

More of the New Covenant

The command to return good for evil and to love enemies is set to the now-familiar refrain: "You have heard . . . but I say to you." The verses need careful study. The following notes may clarify some details.

Verse 38. The principle of "an eye for an eye" came from the Babylonian law-code of Hammurabi in the twentieth century B.C. Its purpose was to restrain vengeance. The Jews adopted this principle for their own Law (see Exodus 21:24; Leviticus 24:19-20; Deuteronomy 19:21). It was also a principle of Roman law in Jesus' time. Jewish courts often permitted a payment of money instead of physical violence, but the basis was still retribution.

Verse 40. The "coat" was a Jewish undergarment with sleeves. The "cloak" was an outer garment, also used as a cover for sleeping. For a poor man to give up both would leave him naked. No wonder we must ask whether Jesus' teaching is practical.

Verse 41. The word "forces" referred to military demands upon civilians. A soldier might require a Jew to transport his baggage.

---

[2] *Ibid.*, pp. 180, 182.

Verse 43. The Jewish Law said: "You shall love your neighbor as yourself" (Lev. 19:18). It did not say: "Hate your enemy." But the word neighbor generally referred to a fellow Israelite. So Jesus demands love beyond the Law.

Verse 46. Tax collectors (publicans) were the despised Jews who worked for Roman overlords in gouging their people. The word became a symbol for the greedy and disloyal. Jesus sometimes offended highly moral people by befriending tax collectors.

Now we are ready to see the impact of the passage as it mounts up to the crashing climax: "You, therefore, must be perfect, as your heavenly Father is perfect." What are we to do with that?

Surely no New Year's resolution, however determined, will make us perfect. Not even the most sincere prayer will succeed here. There are some arguments about the translation of the word perfect. Some translate it (with Luke) as merciful, mature, or all-inclusive (in goodwill). But none of these words softens the impact: you are to be like the holy God.

Such a statement, reinforced with the detailed instructions that Jesus gives, is hard to take. There are two common ways to dodge its difficulties: (1) Water it down. Say: "Jesus was a good fellow. He didn't quite mean that. He was exaggerating for effect. If we're moderately generous, we're O.K." (2) Do the opposite. Interpret it so literally that it doesn't apply to you. After all, nobody ever demanded your cloak or forced you to go a mile.

Both dodges are familiar—and hypocritical. These "hard sayings" of Jesus were meant to be hard. So let's face them.

First, then, we see that their significance is not the bare, literal meaning for a few specific cases. Jesus was not providing a new law book. He was using specific examples to convey a total way of life.

But, second, the examples were deliberately chosen to present a strenuous demand. Maybe Jesus did not expect men, in actual fact, to give away their clothes until they were naked; he did mean that we should love and forgive completely. His beliefs led him to a crucifixion, in which he forgave completely.

Hence Dr. Fosdick says: "He was deliberately presenting a way of life so demanding that no legalism could define it, no unredeemed heart practice it, no saint perfectly fulfill it."[3]

What then? Recognition of that truth is the entry point into the Christian gospel. The report is that Socrates once said: "I have never done anything that was wrong in my private life or in my public life." And Socrates had lived honestly and bravely enough to shame most of us. But Socrates had never confronted the standard of purity that Jesus presents. And we who have, dare not echo Socrates' words. We approach God with the prayer of forgiveness, taught us by our Lord. Every time we celebrate the Holy Communion we mark the fact that the blood of the New Covenant was shed for the forgiveness of sin.

Hence one of America's best known philosophers has written: "The Christian gospel produced a spiritual reorientation of ancient ways and ideals. For the rigidity of the law it substituted the life of the spirit; it scorned the cautious wisdom of the sage to bless the trusting faith of a child; from the beauty of the flesh it turned to the beauty of holiness; it regarded man as a prodigal son and a lost sheep, lost but for the grace of the Divine Shepherd."[4]

But the faith in forgiveness does not relieve us of our mission. It confronts us with the love of God and impels us to make that love real. Notice the reason for loving enemies: "that you may be sons of your Father who is in heaven." (See Matthew 5:45 and John 1:12.) No other reward. Often even good Christians have thought this inadequate. In the early church it was sometimes said, "Love your enemies, and you will have no enemies."

---

[3] *The Man from Nazareth* by Harry Emerson Fosdick, p. 106. Harper & Row, Publishers, Inc., 1949. Used by permission.

[4] *The Moral Ideals of Our Civilization* by Radoslav A. Tsanoff, p. 35. E. P. Dutton & Co., Inc., 1942. Used by permission.

But the Jesus whose enemies crucified him and bade us welcome persecution did not say that. Even Paul missed the point when, quoting the book of Proverbs instead of Jesus, he saw a chance to score a point by helping enemies (Romans 12:20). Jesus asks the purest of motives. In one sense, God is already our father. Yet by loving we become sons of God. So we sometimes say to a young man, "Be a real son of your father!"

An old story in the Jewish Talmud tells how, when the Egyptians were drowning in the Red Sea, the angels joined the children of Israel in their rejoicing. Then God stopped the angels, saying: "What? My children are drowning and ye would rejoice?"

Jesus would have us be like God.

Being Honest with Ourselves

Confucius was once asked whether one should respond to injury with kindness. His answer was: "With what then will you recompense kindness? Recompense injury with justice and recompense kindness with kindness."

Before we feel superior to Confucius, we had better pause to be honest. He has not reached Christ, but he has gone farther than we often go. We are likely to respond to injury with vengeance. The ancient Jewish Law, which Jesus transformed, aimed to limit vengeance. Instead of unrestricted feuding and revenge, the Law set up a standard of just retribution—inflicting a punishment equal to the crime, "an eye for an eye and a tooth for a tooth." If we live up to that, or even to the precept of Confucius, we must often curb our desires.

Indeed, in our hardened world where slaughter has become so common, we scarcely have enough sympathy to love our allies. During the Korean war, it is reported, inexperienced American troops confronted war's horror in the form of a mound of bloody corpses by the roadside. "Don't get shook up," their sergeant said. "They're just Koreans." Allies, but not our own folks. Not important. Don't blame the sergeant. He had more reason to be hardened than we at home. Didn't we do the same? Didn't we react differently to Korean casualties and American casualties? As for loving enemies—say the Communists of China and Russia—who thinks much or prays much about that?

Bertrand Russell, no Christian, expressed admiration for those who really love their enemies and their persecutors. He wrote: "There is nothing to be said against [the Christian principle] except that it is too difficult for most of us to practice sincerely."[5] Such honesty is certainly better than a false pretense about following Jesus, while we go our vindictive ways.

What We Can Do

With all our failings, we are not helpless. The spirit of Christ can make a difference in us. Let's be honest in acknowledging our wrongs, but let's be sincere about our discipleship.

Men can forgive. They can love their enemies. Granted the resentments that we all feel from time to time, the question is: What will we do about them? Will we let them erupt in violent antagonisms, or seethe inside us until they produce ulcers or nervous breakdowns or plain misery? Or will we find that Christ's spirit can move us to turn hatred to love? We can nurse our anger, cherish our vindictiveness. Or we can come clean and find peace with God and ourselves, and even with our enemies. When we are most disappointed in others we can say, with the old African pastor in Alan Paton's novel, "God forgives us. Who am I, not to forgive?"

Even warfare need not destroy love. True, it often does. In the Second World War an American general said: ". . . we must hate. . . . We must lust for battle; our object in life must be to kill." And a newspaper columnist, admitting it would be

---

[5] A History of Western Philosophy by Bertrand Russell, p. 579. Copyright 1945 by Bertrand Russell. Used by permission of Simon and Schuster, Inc.

"a messy task," demanded "total obliteration of Germany as a nation." But a rabbi in the first winter after the war, grieved by the Nazi destruction of his people, nevertheless gave his money to German relief, saying: "I believe with all my heart that we should rise above hatreds and prejudices and succor all people who are afflicted and heavy-laden."

On the one hand we have seen Mussolini call for "that cold, conscious, implacable hate, hate in every home, which is indispensable for victory." On the other hand we have seen a great (and more successful) national leader say, while war still raged:

"With malice toward none; with charity for all; with firmness in the right, as God gives us to see the right, let us strive on to finish the work we are in; to bind up the nation's wounds; to care for him who shall have borne the battle, and for his widow and his orphan—to do all which may achieve and cherish a just, and a lasting peace, among ourselves, and with all nations."[6]

A Controversial Area

So far we have avoided one fair question. How sincere is forgiveness of enemies if we go on fighting them? Does not Jesus demand repudiation of punishment, coercion, and warfare?

Here we enter into an area of honest Christian controversy. It is not so important to argue one side of the question as to see both sides fairly, so that the Christian conscience can decide.

To begin, it is generally agreed that Jesus was not giving advice on how to run a government. He was proclaiming the perfect ethic of God's kingdom, for which he taught men to pray. He said nothing of police, public laws, enforced justice. He gave us, instead of advice on the changing problems of government, the eternal will of God in its utter purity. He does not answer all our questions; he gives us light in which we can look for answers.

---

[6] From Abraham Lincoln's Second Inaugural Address.

He addressed men living under a foreign conqueror. Don't think that makes his message easier. It is hard to forgive an enemy who oppresses you daily. But years later, when Christians had responsibility for government, they had to ask: Now what shall we do?

One voice in the church said: To follow Christ means to reject the ways of the state. Its laws are not entirely just; it jails criminals; it fights national enemies. Another voice said: Even so, it is worse to abandon responsibility for government than to take part in it. Rather use political power—though it be far from Christ's perfection—than abandon it to men of no Christian faith.

The second has clearly been the majority voice since the fourth century. But the minority has continued, sometimes in monasteries, sometimes in the world, to turn aside from the contests of power politics in order to remind men of the purity of God's kingdom.

Sometimes the two groups, in arguing with each other, forget how much they have in common. For both put love above hate; both would rather redeem than destroy their enemies; both see the difference between God's kingdom and the kingdoms of this world.

Now history under God's providence has reached the era of perpetual emergency, when man's age-old sin combined with his new technology threatens the survival of the human race. Even the most violent of men must recognize that there can be no satisfaction in destroying an enemy by thermonuclear weapons while he is destroying us. But the world is caught in the mood of bitter, tragic necessity. The Sermon on the Mount offers no program to present to Congress or the United Nations. But something of its vision and daring, combined with wise statecraft, offer the only hope for mankind.

8 : THE LORD'S PRAYER

From the Sermon on the Mount read Matthew 6:5-15.
For the parallel passage see Luke 11:1-4. ·
To follow up the theme look at Matthew 18:21-35; 26:36-46.

✤ JESUS, immediately after warning his hearers not to "heap up empty phrases," goes on to give them a prayer that has been muttered as empty phrases more times than anyone can count. Evidently men still need to learn about prayer.

We have already looked at Jesus' caution against ostentatious prayers. We took up this passage ahead of its proper order because it said so much about the topic of chapter 5, "Light and Secrecy." Now as we come to the same sentences in their regular sequence, we can concentrate on the Lord's Prayer.

The Motives of Prayer

In approaching the Lord's Prayer notice again what Jesus says about the reasons for praying, especially the wrong reasons. In addition to the one wrong motive that we have already noticed —to "be seen by men"—Jesus describes a second. The motive for prayer is not to provide God with information that he lacks. Critics of prayer often remark that they see no value in prayer, because if there is a powerful, personal God, he knows already what we tell him in prayer. Those who say that do not usually realize that Jesus said most of it first. But Jesus drew a different conclusion.

After rejecting these false motives for prayer, Jesus does not go on to say why men should pray. Perhaps he felt that if people do not know the reasons for prayer, there is no use telling them. Perhaps he saw that good reasons cannot be stated so neatly and glibly as bad reasons. His hearers are left to decide for themselves why anyone should pray. They are not left without any clues. They have all of Jesus' life and teaching as a help. They have especially the accounts about his own praying—most notably that night of prayer reported in Matthew 26:36-46.

Jesus' prayer was often solitary prayer, and he recommends praying "in secret." In this "other-directed" culture of ours, solitude is often frightening. People like to do everything in groups. Jesus points to the value—yes, the necessity—of the solitary approach to God. But he sees the need of both solitude and community. The pronouns of the Lord's Prayer are *our, us, we*—not *my, me, I*. This prayer is for the community of disciples, united by the same Spirit.

Simple Profundity

Compare the differing contexts of the Lord's Prayer in Matthew and Luke. In both cases Jesus is giving a prayer to the community of disciples. They memorized it and passed it on to the church.

The differing translations of Jesus' Aramaic into Greek and the liturgical uses of the prayer in the church led to the two Greek versions. The variations sometimes help clarify the meaning. The likenesses show the essential fidelity of both versions to Jesus' original teaching, the exact Aramaic words of which we cannot know.

Few prayers are shorter or use simpler language than the Lord's Prayer. The whole prayer can be read aloud in seconds. In Matthew's record (as translated in the Revised Standard Version) about three out of four words are monosyllables—an achievement few modern stylists can rival.

Yet the simplicity may be deceptive. The understanding of

the prayer involves all of Jesus' message and the depths of our own spirits. The words carry a weight of meaning from the whole gospel. We see this when we examine the petitions.

Our Father Who Art in Heaven

Augustine says that the opening words are already the answer to the prayer, for we can ask nothing greater than to approach the Lord of the universe as Father. There is still something breathtaking in the idea. Think of the universe of modern physics and astronomy, a universe of uncounted galaxies and mysterious cosmic rays, a universe of distances measured in light years. Then address the creator, "Our Father."

Many a modern man looks at this universe in bewilderment, convinced that it has nothing to do with human hopes and that he means nothing to it. That word, nothing, has become one of the basic words of contemporary philosophy and literature. In his famous short story, "A Clean, Well-Lighted Place," Ernest Hemingway made a parody of the Lord's Prayer, built on the Spanish word nada, meaning nothingness: "Our nada who are in nada, nada be thy name. . . ."

Against that experience of nothingness, known in ancient times as in modern, Christ bids us come to God the Father. The word father occurs seventeen times in the Sermon on the Mount. Further, it has the intimate meaning given it by Jesus' whole ministry. Hence Paul, though in Judaism he had learned to call God Father, felt that because of Christ he could approach the Father in the spirit of an adopted son, not of a slave (Romans 8:15-17).

Nevertheless it is a God of majesty with whom we have this intimate relation. His name is to be hallowed. That is, he is to be approached in his holiness. The tremendous reverence of the Old Testament here enters into the heritage of the Christian.

For thus says the high and lofty One
    who inhabits eternity, whose name is Holy:

"I dwell in the high and holy place,
    and also with him who is of a contrite and humble spirit,
to revive the spirit of the humble,
    and to revive the heart of the contrite."
                                    —Isaiah 57:15.

This is the God whom we approach as Father, whose name we hallow. To "repeat the Lord's Prayer" irreverently is to contradict its very words.

God's Kingdom—and Daily Bread

"Thy kingdom come, thy will be done." The phrases are both petitions and expressions of trust. They call on God, who alone can establish his kingdom. And they call on the praying person to conform to the will of God.

The heart of the prayer, "Thy kingdom come," is the heart (as we have seen) of Jesus' whole message. He bids his disciples pray for that work of God, already beginning but not yet complete. (Recall chapter 2 above.)

Although the kingdom is a gift of God, its practical significance for us is clear in the petition, "Thy will be done, on earth as it is in heaven." The citizens of God's heavenly kingdom are called to live by God's will on earth. That, we may say, should be the normal expectation of any religious commitment. But here, set in the midst of the Sermon on the Mount, it is a call to daring life. We have already read of purity of heart and mercy, of persecution for righteousness' sake, of men lighting the world for God's glory, of love for enemies. All this is the will of God. For this we pray whenever we join Christ in his prayer.

"Give us this day our daily bread." Immediately the prayer turns from the exalted and the strenuous to the commonplace. What is so common as daily bread? Here in the midst of language about the holiness of God and the wonder of his kingdom is the prayer for bread—one of man's ordinary needs.

Believers in some highly "spiritual" religions are ashamed to pray for material things. But the Bible does not despise the material. It assumes that personality is psychosomatic, that God provides for all of life. To pray for bread—for oneself and the world—is as basic to the Christian as to pray, "Hallowed be thy name."

When the disciples first learned this prayer, they did not know that the day was coming when their Lord would offer them bread, saying, "This is my body." In Christian faith it is as natural to pray for bread as to use this same commonplace bread in the sacrament of the Lord's Supper.

Forgive Us Our Debts

Luke says sins (trespasses in the older translations) where Matthew says debts. The difference is unfortunate for the common worship of Christians, since denominations vary in their usage. But the meaning is not difficult. Both words probably come from the same original Aramaic word. The exact meaning is determined less by the specific word than by the entire message of Jesus. For what do Christians seek forgiveness? For the wrongs they have done and for the anger, lust, and pride that prompted the wrongs. They ask forgiveness for every failure of love, for their own unreadiness to forgive.

Anyone who has read the Sermon on the Mount up to this point will not be surprised by the prayer for forgiveness. Once again we see that the New Covenant is a covenant of grace (chapter 6). We meet its terms not by perfect compliance with God's will, but by accepting in faith his forgiveness.

This faith will prompt us to forgive. In Matthew's account, the prayer is followed by the foreboding words of verses 14-15. (See also Matthew 18:21-35.) The idea is not that God is only as generous as we are. The gospel often refutes that idea. But if we refuse to forgive, we lack the faith that can accept forgiveness.

Deliver Us from Evil

"Lead us not into temptation." This is the one petition of the Lord's Prayer that causes confusion because of its wording. The New English Bible translates, "Do not bring us to the test." Either translation is justifiable, and both raise frequent questions. Does a good God deliberately tempt us? If he wants to test us, should we pray that he not do so?

Here, as in some other sayings of Jesus, we can get help from the scholars who translate the Greek back into the probable Aramaic words of Jesus. Then the sentence means this: "Do not allow us to be led into temptation." Or it may mean: "Do not let us be tested beyond our capacity to endure." That is, God is not the tempter; but he has put us into a world of temptations.

In this world we may prayerfully seek to avoid temptations. But what is more important, we pray that we shall not yield to them, that God will deliver us from the evils into which we might be tempted.

Paul in 1 Corinthians 10:13 helps us to understand the issue: "No temptation has overtaken you that is not common to man. God is faithful, and he will not let you be tempted beyond your strength, but with the temptation will also provide the way of escape, that you may be able to endure it."

Life is full of temptations. Many men, meeting temptations in faith and prayer, have found God delivering them.

Thine Is the Glory

Christians often conclude the Lord's Prayer with the words: "For thine is the kingdom and the power and the glory, forever. Amen."

This final doxology or paean of praise does not appear in the oldest manuscripts of the New Testament. By the second century, we know, Christians were using it widely. It echoes earlier themes in the prayer: it hallows God's name and it ascribes to him lordship in his kingdom. Probably Jesus did not include these words; the early church added them, in accord with the general liturgical practice of ending public prayers with an expression of praise.

Amen simply means truly, verily, or may it certainly be so.

When Christians pray this prayer with a genuine Amen, they glorify God. Dr. E. F. Scott in his book, *The Lord's Prayer*, says that, while the church has often drawn up creeds to define loyalty, Christ gave his followers a prayer rather than a creed. Often Christians, separated by doctrines and ecclesiastical authorities, have been able to unite in this prayer. That is appropriate, since the prayer comes from Christ himself.

9 : THE DEMAND FOR DECISION

From the Sermon on the Mount read Matthew 6:19-24.

For the parallel passages see Luke 12:33-34; 11:34-36; 16:13.

To follow up the theme look at Matthew 16:24-26; 1 Timothy 6:17-19; James 5:1-3.

DECISION is a common word. We speak of decisive and indecisive personalities. We say, "I dread to make this decision," or "I made the wrong decision," or "I can't stand indecision."

Some decisions can be postponed or avoided forever. If you are asked to choose between strawberry or chocolate sodas, you may say that you don't want a soda—or you may choose pineapple. If someone asks whether you agree with Einstein's last set of equations, you may dodge a decision; probably neither the world nor you will be worse off.

But some decisions cannot be avoided. William James called

them "forced options," because the nature of the situation forces us to a choice. In such a case, even to delay is to make a decision. The automobile driver, confronted with a sudden hazard must decide whether to use his brakes or not. To wait another hour before deciding is, in effect, to decide against using the brakes. The young man, considering whether to propose marriage, must choose. To put off the choice for a few years usually means negative decision.

The Bible confronts us with a forced option. Jesus says, "Follow me." He attracts us. But so do some other forces. We maneuver pathetically to delay or to find a "both-and" answer. Jesus comes back insisting that it's "either-or." If throughout the years we keep saying, "Let's think this over a little longer before doing something rash," some day we will waken to realize that the Master has kept moving, while the unconscious decisions of everyday life were moving us in the opposite direction.

The Uncompromising God

When Christianity came to northern Europe, rulers sometimes led whole armies through rivers for mass baptisms. As the story goes, some warriors walked into the water with the right hand held high and dry. The soul could belong to God; but the unbaptized right hand could wield a sword as freely as before.

Our own story may be like that. We pledge loyalty to God, but withhold something dear. Some bad habit, pet vanity, ambition, or bank account remains unbaptized, uncommitted. So we try to serve God with half the heart, soul, mind, and strength.

This is an old story in human history. It is a recurring theme in the life of Israel. Moses, leading his people out of bondage, found them, on the one hand, longing for God and freedom, on the other hand, yearning for a golden calf or the fleshpots of Egypt. In the promised land Joshua confronted them with the

words, "Choose this day whom you will serve," and heard them
answer that they would choose the Lord (Joshua 24:14-28).

But the people found new gods in the new land. So the time
came when Elijah demanded of them, "How long will you go
limping with two different opinions? If the Lord is God, follow
him; but if Baal, then follow him" (1 Kings 18:21). Then the
great prophets, one after another, called the people from their
indecision to loyalty. Often they likened Israel to an unfaith-
ful wife, pledged to one husband but ready to yield to the
temptations of other lovers.

Now Jesus appears and calls for a clear decision. You cannot
keep wavering, he tells men. Time is running out. You must
take a stand.

Not many heed him. First, people try to ignore him and go on
as before. But he can't be ignored. So they try to accept him,
and give him a bit of their loyalty. One Roman emperor, Alex-
ander Severus, includes him among the several gods of his
private chapel.

And there he remains, for thousands of people, to this day.
They count him as one of the leaders they can use. They want
his blessing along with all the other blessings of life. They call
religion one interest in a well-rounded life.

But he will not allow it so. For he comes to us from that God,
who almost alone among ancient gods, would tolerate no rivals
—the God who said from Sinai: "You shall have no other gods
before me . . . . for I the LORD your God am a jealous God. . ."
(Exod. 20:3, 5). This God reigns while the compromising gods
are forgotten. And when men today seek to give him part of
their allegiance, they do it at the risk of tearing their inmost
selves apart.

The Specific Issue: God or Mammon

When it comes to stating the issue specifically, Jesus could
not have put it more directly for us. "You cannot serve God

and mammon." Mammon—let's face it—means wealth of every kind. Translators have used various phrases: profit, money, gain, the almighty dollar.

Was Jesus specifically foreseeing American civilization? Why, we may wonder, couldn't he have used a different contrast? It would be so much nicer if he had said, "You cannot serve God and Caesar." Or God and the Sanhedrin. Or God and Baal. Then we could happily nod agreement, forgetting that we too have our Caesars and Sanhedrins and Baals. But he puts it so we cannot dodge it. He hits us at our sorest spot.

Has ever a nation been more entranced by mammon than ours? Walter Marshall Horton once brought back from Europe a photograph of the "American suite" in a hotel of Prague, Czechoslovakia. On the wall was a large tapestry of the American dollar. Dr. Horton suggests that its purpose was to assist the nightly devotions of pious dollar-worshiping tourists. We sometimes openly boast that the mainspring of our society is the profit motive. If so, says Jesus, we are headed for damnation. The apostle echoes Jesus when he writes: "For the love of money is the root of all evils; it is through this craving that some have wandered away from the faith and pierced their hearts with many pangs" (1 Tim. 6:10).

The Value of Material Things

It is possible—though not likely for us—to misunderstand Jesus here. He is not one of the many religious teachers who believe that matter is inherently evil, that the spiritual life should avoid material things so far as possible. He believes, with the Old Testament, that God created the universe and called it good, that God gave man dominion over the things of nature and expected man to enjoy them. Christianity has fought off these religions and heresies which called creation evil. William Temple, a great Archbishop of Canterbury, surprised many people when he wrote that Christianity is "the most avowedly materialistic of all the great religions," because it neither ignores nor denies the material, but asserts its reality and its subordination to God's purpose.

So we should enjoy and use the material goods God has created. There is nothing unhealthy about honest labor—like that in the carpenter shop at Nazareth—to provide for human needs. Martin Luther said that the cobbler who soles the pope's shoes can serve God as truly as the pope who prays for the soul of the cobbler.

All this is true, we have every right to believe. But if these last two paragraphs take the sting out of Jesus' words, they become false and blasphemous. Jesus was intending to make us uncomfortable, not to ease our consciences. Yes, the Christian can use things (or wealth) without serving them. But that is not easy. "For where your treasure is, there will your heart be also."

A key to understanding Jesus lies in a favorite modern word, security. In our vocabulary securities are a type of investment. Jesus is telling us that there is no true security in securities. Our gilt-edged investments, our government bonds cannot give what only God can give.

An insurance company advertises with the motto, "Unforeseen events need not change and shape the course of man's affairs." The slogan is absurd. Of course, insurance is a wonderful invention. It relieves financial distress and enables us to share our insecurities. It may be an expression of love for our dependents. But it can never meet the challenge of unforeseen events. Life insurance does not conquer the challenge of death. "You can't take it with you." Nor will it replace you in a family that loves you. Would a policy on the life of Jesus have softened the cruelty of his crucifixion or enhanced the glory of his resurrection? Does insurance give us peace of mind about H-bombs? Can any wealth assure us that our children will find blessedness in lives of integrity, unharmed by the world's temptations?

There comes a point where we must decide the direction and the basic confidence that will control our lives. We have a saying about trying to carry water on both shoulders. Jesus puts it more bluntly: if we serve mammon, we *despise* God. A strong word! But day in and day out people, including churchmen, do despise God. When a physician turns his back on human need to enjoy a more profitable practice, he despises God. When a youth chooses his lifework, thinking only of what he can get rather than what he can give, he despises God. When a clergyman moves up the social scale by pleasing congregations and dulling the sharp Word of God, he despises God.

An Example

Perhaps we most despise God when, instead of defying him, we "use" him to support our love of mammon. In the great international conflicts of the twentieth century, one American group has proposed a business campaign to save the world. The technique? To "put the money on the line to resell Christian philosophy to America, and thus smother out communism and other false ideologies." For "any idea, even Christian philosophy, can be sold if backed by a proper sales campaign."

So this group proposed an Ideological War Council to "coordinate and thus make effective all of the movements that are now selling partial or watered-down portions of the Sermon on the Mount." It recommended that Roman Catholic, Protestant, and Jewish leaders combine to prepare a credo. Then five of the top advertising men of the land should prepare these truths "for sale." Such an effort, blessed by God, would spread throughout the world. So said the proposal.

America's most famous theologian, Reinhold Niebuhr, commented scathingly on this notion of having the Sermon on the Mount "neatly packaged and 'sold' by salesmen and advertisers. What kind of blindness or perversity prompts this vapid idealism to choose, of all symbols, the Sermon on the Mount, with its exacting moral demands, all of them straining at the limits of human possibilities? What will the 'Ideological War Council' do with the words, 'Lay not up for yourselves treasures upon earth, where moth and rust doth corrupt'?"[1]

But don't we all commit this sin? Don't we want to use the Christian faith to win our ideological wars, instead of letting it humble and transform us?

The Wider Issue

Throughout much of life we try to serve two masters. Mental hospitals harbor the worst schizophrenics, victims of personality disintegration. But the rest of us, too, need healing.

Perhaps we are like Augustine, enjoying his youthful lusts and praying, "God, make me a Christian—but not yet."

The famous novelist Lillian Smith has described with rare memory and insight an aspect of her own childhood.[2] Like all children she asked questions that adults could not answer. She remembers also questions that she felt she did not dare ask. Some, she says, "I could not whisper even to myself." They were rooted in a deep uneasiness.

"I can still feel our anxiety as we were taught conflicting beliefs which we could not live and yet which we dared not admit, even to ourselves, that we did not live. I cannot forget the feeling of that never-ending struggle in our minds between democracy and white supremacy that wore down our energy and strength and compelled us to put up signs in our own souls, segregating beliefs so that one could live in peace with one's self.

"It was a false peace, yes; for splitting a child or a nation or a world into fragments and trying to wall up the fragments is hardly the way to avoid conflict."

Miss Smith is describing a problem that concerns all of us. Recent psychology has shown us that, often without our knowledge, we are torn in our subconscious levels by the opposition

---

[1] *Christianity and Crisis*, March 19, 1951.
[2] *Christianity and Crisis*, July 10, 1950.

between contrary commitments. Deeply imbedded in our emotional lives are symbols like democracy, equality, Christianity, love, service. Conflicting with them are counter-drives: ambition, prestige, comfort, financial security. So personalities are torn apart in this uneasy age.

It is dangerous to follow Christ. But once we have met him, it is also dangerous to resist him.

10 : TRUST AND ANXIETY

From the Sermon on the Mount read Matthew 6:25-34; 7:7-11.
For the parallel passages see Luke 12:22-31; 11:9-13.
To follow up the theme look at 2 Corinthians 12:7-10; Philippians 4:6-7.

HERE is the heart of the Sermon on the Mount. Here Jesus confronts life's deepest personal problem.

We start with a scripture passage that seems unbelievable. The language is familiar and beautiful. It was originally poetry, and something of the poetic quality lingers in our translations. The words are often set to music and sung. People love to hear them. All this helps to make the language so ethereal that most people never bother to ask what it means. If they do investigate the meaning, they may take one startled look, then run away. It's beautiful, they think, but oh, how impractical!

Yet if we can get beneath the surface and penetrate the real depths of the message, we will not dismiss it so lightly. We will find it catching us at a sensitively sore spot. The chances are that we have found all kinds of fluff and padding to protect the soreness. This message will rip off these futile coverings. But then, if by the grace of God we do respond, it will heal the wound so that the old protections are unnecessary.

This Age of Anxiety

This is the age when fantastic science fiction turns into fact overnight. Astronauts, satellites, and space exploration are part of the daily news. To have some fun and to educate the public at the same time, the Hayden Planetarium in New York once offered to take reservations for space trips. Forms were prepared and prospective travelers checked the tour they wished.

The applications rolled in by the thousands. Some, of course, were just keeping up the joke. But someone started asking why so many people replied. The most realistic answer seemed to be that worried and weary people wanted a chance, though it was only an imaginary one, to escape from the troubles and worries of life. One applicant wrote: "It would be heaven to get away from this busy earth. I honestly wish God would let me go somewhere where it's nice and peaceful, good, safe, and secure."

That's one of the signs of the times. There are many more. A book by one of our most famous poets is called *Age of Anxiety*. That title reflects the judgment of many. A book called *Peace of Mind* sold hundreds of thousands of copies in the 1940's. Then came a wave of other best sellers with titles like *Peace of Soul, How to Stop Worrying and Start Living, A Guide to Confident Living, Identity and Anxiety*. The books in this field range from profound helpfulness to slick absurdities. But they are evidence of the pathetic eagerness of the mid-twentieth century to get away from its fears and anxieties.

Even young people—supposedly the eager, venturesome group in society—show the same signs. Many a survey claims to show that, whether in business or politics or a choice of a career, youth is more eager for security than for adventure. The "hot rodders" are a minority. The beatniks, despite some notorious antics, are a far more troubled group than the "flaming youth" of the "flapper age." In one eastern college the students, far above average in wealth and brains, spent a year deciding the subject for a week's religious program and came up with the title, "Anxiety, Despair and Faith: the Search for Meaning in Life."

This is no occasion for the old pastime of bemoaning "the younger generation." Its lack of confidence is part of its realism and may be the gateway to wisdom.

Of course, there are plenty of noisy, cocksure people to tell us that these "signs of the times" are exaggerated. But the blustering is pretty clearly a cover-up for the emptiness underneath. A European artist, visiting America, said that he liked this country, but found some difficulty getting adjusted. "Naturally one needs constant practice," he reported. "It is not a simple matter to keep repeating daily: 'Yes, everything is fine.'"

The artist is not the only one who has seen through some of our typical false bravado. Wise news analysts have referred to the "emotional binges" that America has gone through in connection with certain military and political crises. Level-headed people have shown how our reactions to national and international dangers have often been hysterically unintelligent. Al Capp, the famous cartoonist, has observed that we are so insecure that we dare not laugh at ourselves. Yes, America knows anxiety.

Can Christ Help Us?

No doubt Jesus is talking about our problems when he tells us not to be anxious. But is his advice good? Take a long look at that passage in Matthew. Try to see exactly what it means. Can anybody really believe this? Is there anything harder to believe?

There the words used are mostly words of only one or two syllables—such words as life, food, body, clothing, birds, lilies, and grass. And that word anxious, five times in one paragraph.

And promises, beautiful but incredible: God will look after you; your prayers will be answered.

Some of the sentences are so easy to refute that we wonder how anyone could make them. "Ask, and it will be given you; seek, and you will find; knock, and it will be opened to you." Who cannot demolish that promise from his own experience? Who has not had prayers unanswered and yearnings frustrated? Or look at the words, "Consider the lilies of the field. . . ." Their idyllic beauty charms people. But then reality takes hold. Marx and Engels, the fathers of modern communism, write with bitter sarcasm: "Yes, consider the lilies of the field, how they are eaten by goats, transplanted by man into his button-hole." Against our will, we grant that they have made a point.

So we become realistic. We count on our own achievements. Maybe God can feed and clothe us, we think, but look how much better modern agriculture and industry do the job. This is a modern world and a hard world, and if you don't take care of yourself, no one will do it for you.

But the haunting words of Jesus will not quite leave us. As we think further, we realize that he knew something about life. He met disappointments. He told parables of injustices. He yearned to escape a cruel death, and did not have his way. And his words were preserved for us by disciples who knew the hard side of life. They must have seen something in his promises that we don't see.

And our proud modern answers have not always been so good. Anxiety does shake us to the depths. We haven't solved all our problems. The last president of the League of Nations Assembly, Norwegian Carl Hambro, said in 1935: "Here in Geneva we have every fear but the fear of God." He had a point. In declaring our independence of God we ran into some real troubles. With all that modern nutrition and medicine can do there comes the time when no one can add an inch to his stature or a day to his span of life.

The Basis of It All

Several things Jesus clearly does *not* mean. He is *not* patting us on the back and saying, "Don't worry. Everything will come out all right." He knew things do not always turn out "all right." He is *not* saying that God will step in to correct all our follies and omissions. Sometimes he assumes a place for prudent foresight (Luke 14:28-30). He is *not* saying that those who trust God will never be injured or persecuted. He has already told men to expect, and rejoice in, persecution. He is *not* saying we should ignore food. He has bidden us pray for daily bread and he has never criticized honest work. He is *not* saying that the lilies and the grass will live happily ever after. As he spoke those words, he probably thought of one of his favorite Old Testament books, which said: "The grass withers, the flower fades; but the word of our God will stand for ever" (Isa. 40:8).

Now we can see what Jesus *does* say. He tells us that our destinies are controlled by the God who stands forever. That we, who determine neither our births nor our deaths, are helpless; but that if we trust God, we tie our feebleness to an eternal power and purpose. That if the goal of life is to keep the heart beating and the stomach expanding, we all fail before long. But that if we seek first God's kingdom and his righteousness, we will be given all else that we need—not immunity to hunger and pain and death, but confidence in spite of them.

Put this in terms of our modern psychology. Dr. Rollo May, in his widely-read book, *Man's Search for Himself,* says that the clinical practice of psychologists today shows that the chief problem of people is *emptiness.* By emptiness he means lack of purpose, lack of power, lack of direction. And he finds more anxiety today than in any period of history since the breakdown of the Middle Ages.

Now see how the Christian gospel fits this problem. When we are detached from God, trying to be self-sufficient, everything threatens our existence. We are finite, mortal. War or an invisible virus can wipe us out. In our nakedness and peril there is nothing to hold on to. But, says Jesus, trust your Father. Your life gets its power, its vitality, its meaning from him. Neither war nor virus nor any other thing threatens God. You are secure because your security is in him.

This is not the Stoic fatalism which many people adopt these days. It does not say, "Since you cannot do anything about it, you may as well face it with a minimum of emotion." No, Jesus' word is positive. *Trust overcomes anxiety.*

Are you approaching pain or death? Countless men have met both. Empty men have been overwhelmed with anxiety; trusting men have been confident.

Some Examples

This Christian faith is not just something "up in the air." It makes a difference in life.

H. G. Wells rejected the Christian faith. For years he was an optimist, confident that the human race could lick its problems and move on to ever greater triumphs without any help from an obsolete God. But events chipped away at his confidence. The emptiness of his faithlessness left him helpless before the anxiety of the twentieth century. So at the end of the trail he was helpless. Man, he wrote, is played out. He goes to his doom. Perhaps some other animal will come along "better adapted to face the fate that closes in more and more swiftly upon mankind."

Martin Luther heard and believed Christ's answer to anxiety. Though he had his days of terrible doubts, faith rose up in him to conquer despair. He was challenged once by a Cardinal who threatened him with all the power of the pope, whose little finger was stronger than all of Germany. "Where then," thundered the Cardinal, "will a wretched worm like you be?" "Then as now," said Luther, "in the hands of Almighty God."

It happens today too. Out of Soviet-occupied Germany once came a letter worth quoting, from a Christian student. "The greatness of the power of God had never been more clearly revealed to us, and could hardly be better expressed, than in the following somewhat desperate statement made in a meeting of the Communist youth: 'We cannot get a hold on them; they always hide behind their God,' or in a remark made in a discussion as to whether convinced materialists should be sent into the *Studentengemeinde* in order to try to win over its members and thus create division among them: 'It is dangerous; they come back as Christians.'"

Answers to Prayer

Now we can see clearly why Jesus is so confident that prayers will be answered. "Ask, and it will be given you." If we evil folk give good gifts to our children, the heavenly Father will do far more for us. But what will God give us? Not any old thing we happen to want. The answer is the theme of the whole Sermon on the Mount. God grants us his kingdom. So when Jesus prayed at Gethsemane, he was granted, not release from the pain ahead, but the power of God "strengthening him" (Luke 22:43). So when Paul prayed for release from his "thorn in the flesh," he got the divine answer, "My grace is sufficient for you" (2 Cor. 12:7-10). No wonder Paul could write his friends that the answer to their "anxiety" was "the peace of God, which passes all understanding" (Phil. 4:6-7). It was no easy peace of mind, free of trouble; it was God's peace, known best in struggle. And that is the only peace that satisfies the soul.

Now perhaps we are ready to understand a great liturgical prayer of the church, which we may have heard and wondered about often:

"O Lord our God, who art always more ready to bestow thy good gifts upon us than we are to seek them, and art willing to give more than we desire or deserve: help us so to seek that we may truly find, so to ask that we may joyfully receive, so to knock that the door of thy mercy may be opened unto us; through Jesus Christ our Lord."

11 : THE PERILS OF JUDGING

From the Sermon on the Mount read Matthew 7:1-6.
For the parallel passages see Luke 6:37-38, 41-42.
To follow up the theme look at John 8:1-11; Romans 2:1-4.

🐝 THE MOST FAMOUS louse in all history is the one
Robert Burns saw on the hat of the proud woman sitting in
front of him in church. In amusement he watched its crawlings,
which the "fine" lady knew nothing about. And he put his
thoughts in the lines,

> Oh wad some Pow'r the giftie gie us
> To see oursels as ithers see us!

But actually we normally prefer *not* to see ourselves as others
see us. We prefer to keep our own picture of the self. So someone has revised Burns' lines to read:

> Oh wad some power to ithers gie,
> To see myself as I see me.

In either case the problem is evident. We share the common
human failing of passing judgments on other people—judgments
in which our own pride and defensiveness take the place of understanding. At the same time they, we know, are passing judgments on us. We worry about their judgments. More often
than we admit or even realize, as we go through the day's paces,
the subconscious levels of personality are saying tormentingly to
us, "What will they think of me?"

We can build a cruel and miserable world in this process.
Even when we are eager for friendship, we find ourselves sizing

each other up. Often one of the great embarrassments of court-ship is having to meet his (or her) family. Justifiably or not, there is the feeling that we meet them, not to make friends, but to pass in review and be judged. And those parents are equally uneasy as they face the scrutiny of this young person who has won the interest of their son (or daughter). In a moment walls may arise that will take months or years to melt away.

Going through life, we have to "make a good impression." It's such a job that sometimes we must even try—this is really curious—try to be natural. The one thing that logically should take no special effort seems more than we can accomplish. But we are making warped judgments of others. . . . they are making warped judgments of us. . . . we are making warped judgments of ourselves. . . . and no one can break the cycle of vicious judgments. . . . and no one quite realizes how vicious they are.

"Judge Not . . ."

In this situation Jesus says, "Judge not, that you be not judged." The whole network of misery is broken apart with one clear sentence. But is this possible? Every decision of life requires judgments. To take the time to read this chapter involves a judgment as to the use of your time—and of the relative values of the institutions and persons who make demands on your time. We must continually judge, evaluate, criticize, and choose.

Yet we see what Jesus means, as he goes on: "Why do you see the speck that is in your brother's eye, but do not notice the log that is in your own eye?" Among Jesus' listeners the exaggerated language—like that of a tall story—probably provoked a laugh. The speaker in one of his typical ways was using absurd language. But the laugh perhaps gave way to the profound smile of self-recognition. Yes, we do just that. Is something wrong with us? Then let's discover and gloat over a fault, however small, in someone else.

The centuries since Jesus have invented new names for this old experience. Psychologists talk of "projection" and "transfer." People project their inner troubles on society or the universe; they transfer their own guilt feelings into accusations of other people. How often we laugh bitterly at the person who so obviously criticizes in others the very qualities which we resent in him. He sees the speck and misses the log. But, then, we do too.

The apostle Paul says that, whoever you are, you have no excuse for judging another. "For in passing judgment upon him you condemn yourself, because you, the judge, are doing the very same things" (Rom. 2:1). Kierkegaard tells of the thief who stole a hundred dollar note, then saw a second thief swindle it from him. The first thief hauled the second into court and demanded justice. The judge asked the embarrassing question of where the money had come from and found both accuser and accused guilty.

Maybe we resist that way of putting it, saying: "Of course, I'm not perfect. I make my mistakes. But there are some things I don't do and I have a right to complain when someone else does them." But are you sure? You have not murdered. *Have you never hated?* (Matthew 5:21-22)? You have not committed adultery. *Have you remembered Christ's definition of adultery* (Matthew 5:27-28)? You have never sworn falsely under oath. *Have you been utterly sincere* (Matthew 5:33-37)? Every accusation that we make is transferred by Jesus to the deeper level, where no one can proudly claim virtue. "In the moment that you are truly aware of God's presence you certainly would not think of looking at a mote in your brother's eye, nor would you think of applying this terribly strict standard—you who are yourself guilty."[1]

That realization dawned upon a startled group one day. They

---

[1] *Works of Love* by Sören Kierkegaard, translated by D. F. and L. M. Swenson, p. 308. Princeton University Press, 1946. Used by permission.

had caught a woman in the crime of adultery. There was no doubt about it, she was guilty. The law said she should be stoned to death. They brought her to Jesus, told him their story, and put him on the spot. What now would he do with his fine words about forgiveness? Would he ignore a crime clearly defined in the Law of Moses? His answer was as clear as the crime and the Law, and far more profound. "Let him who is without sin among you be the first to throw a stone at her" (John 8:7). Read the rest of the story. See how the shamed crowd drifted away. See how Jesus neither condemned the guilty woman nor made light of the wrong she had done.

Luke puts the words, "Judge not" immediately after the words, "Be merciful, even as your Father is merciful." That helps us to see the point. We cannot stop evaluating, but we can be merciful. We remember that it is the merciful who shall obtain mercy. We who crave mercy can show mercy.

God's Kingdom and Human Government

Again the question of practicability arises. Does not Jesus undermine the possibility of sound civil law and judicial procedure? Forgiveness is beautiful, mercy is lovely. But we cannot let murderers run at large, our mercy thus permitting more murders. What if God does find us all guilty of inner sins? Society must be concerned with overt acts that disrupt peace and justice. In this area some are guilty and some are not.

True. But Jesus too is true. As we have seen before, Jesus gives us the truth of the kingdom of God. He shows us our human life as God sees it. He exposes the hypocrisies and deceptions of life. He does not, in all this, take the place of civil government.

At this crucial point, however, we are not entitled to say: "Oh, that means we can ignore Jesus in politics." A judge, passing sentence on a criminal, might think (as, we know, some judges do think):

"This man before me may be no more guilty before God than I. If I had been in his shoes, I might have done what he did. Only God, not I, can judge his life. I do know that he has violated the laws of society and harmed other people. To prevent his continuing to harm them, society denies him freedom. As the agent of society, I must pronounce the sentence. As I do so, I pray that God may have mercy on his soul and on the souls of all of us."

The governor of an important penal institution has hanging over his mantelpiece a wood carving which says: "Every man is fighting a hard battle; therefore, be merciful." Mercy cannot entirely replace judicial procedures and forceful restraint of lawbreakers. But it can transform justice so that it does not resemble vengeance. It can eliminate the kind of vision that sees specks and ignores beams. It can work to help rather than to humiliate the criminal.

The Need to Discriminate

In Matthew's report the warning against judging is immediately followed by a jolting contrast: "Do not give dogs what is holy; and do not throw your pearls before swine." That puzzling sentence does not seem to fit the development of thought. Matthew is the only New Testament writer to report it. In the early church, we know, it was used to exclude curious spectators from the Lord's Supper, a celebration reserved for those who came in reverent faith.

If the statement belongs here—some scholars doubt it, or consider it part of a lost parable—it is a reminder that all the dangers of judging cannot relieve us of the need to discriminate. Jesus often made this point. He warned his followers against false prophets. He denounced evil. He makes us more intent to discern between good and bad, between seeming good and true good. He awakens a more sensitive conscience, a surer power of evaluation. What he rejects is the impulse to stand in judgment over others, as though we could take God's position and see truly into the lives of our fellowmen.

The warning against judgment has special force when we think of other peoples, especially those for whom we feel some hostility. The tendency of all "in-groups" is to judge "out-groups" harshly. Often such judgments actually endanger the world. Consider a few examples.

1. Some investigators in 1952 set out to discover, through the pollster's techniques, some of the bases of international hostilities. Their findings help us to "see ourselves as others see us." Americans described themselves with such adjectives as peace-loving, generous, intelligent. Foreigners described us as progressive, practical, conceited, domineering. In selecting adjectives to describe themselves, Americans picked thirteen complimentary ones for every uncomplimentary one.

2. Shortly after the war with Japan, the Reverend Mrs. Tamaki Uemura, a distinguished churchwoman and president of the Japanese YWCA, visited the United States. When a New York taxi driver learned she was from Japan, he said: "You folks had better all repent over there. America is always right."

3. An American political scientist studied closely the official propaganda from Russia for several years. He found plenty of criticisms of the policies of other nations, but never a single hint that Russia might ever be wrong. On the other hand, an American news reporter, traveling in a Russian ship, overheard through his porthole a sarcastic conversation between two Russian sailors. One said that in America everything was wonderful and nothing wrong or bad. "Would you like to be there?" he asked the second. "Oh, no," came the answer, "I am sometimes both wrong and bad."

4. Several psychologists and social scientists in 1961 released results of their studies of Soviet-American relations. They reported that each society consistently interprets the actions of

the other in the worst possible way. The result is a pathological inability to communicate.

5. In situations of racial tension, prejudiced people cannot see other people accurately because of stereotypes. The white Gentile, for example, fits the Negro and Jew into his preconceived picture. The facts about persons make very little difference, because those facts are apprehended through the stereotype.

In all these cases, the "beam" in an observer's eye leads him to condemn others without asking about himself.

A Religion of Grace

We have seen before that the Sermon on the Mount leads us to the point where we put our confidence not in our goodness but in God's grace. We dare not judge because we are not fit to judge. In every judgment we condemn ourselves. Even after we have been told this, we continue to judge. Try it for a week and see! You may find Jesus' warning restraining you, and you may find the power of Christian love tempering your judgments. But still, buried deeply in the subconscious foundations of personality where we cannot root it out, is the tendency to go on measuring others, judging them, taking satisfaction in our petty triumphs over others.

Thus our hope lies in God's grace—his forgiving, healing, empowering love. As Augustine put it, "he who thinks he lives without sin puts aside not sin, but pardon." None of us is fit to throw that first stone. But pardon is real. God promises mercy for the merciful.

'Twas a thief that said the last kind word to Christ:
Christ took the kindness and forgave the theft.
                                        —Robert Browning

So the Sermon on the Mount leads us to the message of the cross.

12 : THE GOLDEN RULE

From the Sermon on the Mount read Matthew 7:12.
For the parallel passage see Luke 6:31.
*To follow up the theme look at Leviticus 19:18; Matthew
22:34-40; John 13:34-35.*

🙢 LIFE IS DIFFICULT enough that people often wish they
could find some slogan that would always guide them. The modern yen for getting everything in a cellophane-wrapped package
is not entirely new. Long before there was any cellophane, the
human race learned to love neatly packaged goods. People have
wanted even their religions to come in packages—all in one
container, no loose ends, no puzzling leftovers, nothing unsure.
So they have longed for rules, proverbs, slogans—to save thinking and praying.

But the idea won't work. No rule can do our thinking for us.
In Christian faith no rule can take the place of the personal
encounter with God. Nor can any rule take the place of the
Christian gospel.

Two slogans we often hear, as though nothing else were
needed: "Let your conscience be your guide," and "Follow the
Golden Rule." Each of these, when used in the light of the
whole Christian faith, can be helpful. Each by itself lacks
something.

Look first at conscience. Huckleberry Finn once found himself quite without his intention, helping a runaway slave to escape. His conscience bothered him about disobeying the law,
and his conscience bothered him when he thought about obey-
ing the law and turning the slave in. So he complained:

"It don't make no difference whether you do right or wrong, a person's conscience ain't got no sense, and just goes for him anyway. If I had a yaller dog that didn't know no more than a person's conscience does I would pison him. It takes up more room than all the rest of a person's insides, and yet ain't no good, nohow."[1]

No doubt Huck should have been more grateful for conscience, but what he says has its truth. Conscience approved the crucifixion of Jesus. When Paul accepted Christ, he had to retrain his conscience which had been educated by the strict Jewish Law. When conscience urges us *to do right*, it reflects the God who created us. But when it tells us *what is right*, it reflects also our social conditioning. That is why conscience alone is not enough; it needs the whole Christian faith.

In the same way, the Golden Rule needs the guidance and direction of whole Christian faith.

The Golden Rule in Human History

One reason the Golden Rule is so popular is that it seems to require no specific faith and no specific religious beliefs. Men may argue over many questions, but often they can agree on the Golden Rule. Religious teachers all over the world, many of them long before Jesus, taught one form or another of the Golden Rule. Look at a few examples.

1. The Hindu *Mahabharata* teaches: "Men gifted with intelligence and purified souls should always treat others as they themselves wish to be treated."

2. A Jainist writing, also from India, says: "A man should wander about treating all creatures in the world as he himself would be treated."

3. When Confucius was asked for a single word to sum up the rules of life, he answered: "Is not reciprocity such a word? What you do not want done to yourself, do not do to others."

---

[1] *The Adventures of Huckleberry Finn* by Mark Twain. Chapter 33.

4. The Taoists taught: "Regard your neighbor's gain as your own gain, and regard your neighbor's loss as your own loss."

5. In the generation-before Jesus a man asked the great Rabbi Hillel to teach him the Law while standing on one foot. Hillel answered: "What thou thyself hatest, do not to thy neighbor. This is the whole Law. The rest is commentary. Go and learn it."

Not only the great religions have framed this rule. Some philosophers, unwilling to accept the Christian belief in God's revelation in Christ, have worked out principles of conduct much like the Golden Rule. Thus Immanuel Kant tried to base his ethics simply on the principle of logical consistency. He decided that rationality demands that he act on principles that he could will all other men to act upon.

Now we see why Martin Luther could say that the Golden Rule is part of the "natural law"—the moral law which men can recognize without any Christian teaching. It is in the New Testament, he said, but even the Turk, who is warring against Christianity, understands it. Luther was right. Although the Golden Rule is not in the Koran, another Islamic writing says: "No one of you is a believer until he loves for his brother what he loves for himself."

In chapter 7 we noted that the Emperor Severus included Jesus among the gods in his chapel. This same emperor inscribed the Golden Rule on his palace walls. Maybe it seemed to him a good illustration of his religious tolerance.

But the Golden Rule is not enough.

The Golden Rule Without the Gospel

Look carefully at the next sentence and see whether you agree. *The Golden Rule without the gospel can be (1) a cheap standard of conduct and (2) a source of frustration.* Let's examine both ideas.

(1) The Golden Rule can be a cheap standard of conduct. Let's be grateful that it also may be, whether inside or outside Christianity, a high standard; but it is not always.

For example, suppose you are a person with plenty of ability, well able to look out for yourself. You may say: "I am tough. I believe life is a dog-eat-dog struggle, with everyone out for himself. I ask no mercy and I give none." You can still live by the letter of the Golden Rule. You want no love or forgiveness; you do not extend it to others. The chances are that some day you will awaken to realize your dependence on others; but for years you can live by cheap standards, all the while quoting the Golden Rule.

Or take the case of Thomas Hobbes in the seventeenth century. He may have been a better man than his theory; but if we take him at his word, we find a crude theory of morality. He believed that all men are moved by the restless desire for power. This makes us bitter competitors, each endangering the other. Without some political power controlling us, life would be "solitary, poor, nasty, brutish, and short." Every man naturally has the right to anything he can grab, including the lives of others. But to save our own skins we decide to limit our grasping. We make agreements with our fellowmen. We'll not kill them if they'll not kill us. So Hobbes comes around to quoting the Golden Rule from Jesus. And all for frankly selfish reasons.

Or say that you find in business that the Golden Rule "pays off." So, again selfishly, you may live up to it as strictly as the businessman next door who honestly loves his fellowman.

Or, to take a last example, a moral pervert might use the letter of the Golden Rule to justify involving others in his evil ways. He would gladly have men encourage him in vice, and he will so encourage them.

All this is simply saying what the Sermon on the Mount has been saying to us week after week: No external form of action, no rule is enough.

The Golden Rule cannot be applied legalistically anyway. The child cannot do for the parent what he wants the parent to do for him. The patient doesn't do for the doctor what the doctor does for the patient. The Golden Rule requires the imagination to put oneself in the place of another and see his needs. It requires love.

(2) The Golden Rule can be a source of frustration. Even though, as we have seen, it is not always a very high ethic, it often rises above our normal conduct. Frequently we praise the Golden Rule, then live by some lower code. Someone says, "I'll treat him the way he treated me—tit for tat." (It reminds us of "an eye for an eye, a tooth for a tooth.") Or someone tries the popular slogan, "Do unto others what they would like to do to you, but do it first."

Someone has said, "The Golden Rule works like gravitation." But it doesn't. Gravitation is natural, independent of us. We can't argue with it or disobey it. We do disobey the Golden Rule. History records countless acts of disobedience to it. Our inclinations are to make exceptions of ourselves, to claim privileges—maybe "just this once"—which we do not give. The person of insight knows that often he does not live up to the Golden Rule. Any rule hanging over us, especially a rule that we disobey, is frustrating. To try to obey it and not succeed is even more frustrating.

The Christian gospel is not a set of rules. It is God's gift to us, a gift that awakens a new spirit in us. The spirit takes the frustration away. With the spirit we want to guide our conduct by the Golden Rule. "The written code kills, but the Spirit gives life" (2 Cor. 3:6).

The Golden Rule Within the Gospel

Within the gospel the Golden Rule can become a pathway of life. When the words convey the spirit of the Sermon on the Mount, they become a helpful guide in many a situation. In Luke's Gospel the Golden Rule concludes the paragraph which starts, "Love your enemies." Love, mercy, forgiveness, the spirit of the Beatitudes—here we find the spirit in which Jesus meant the Golden Rule.

Compare the Golden Rule with the other summaries of Jesus' teaching in the Bible readings at the beginning of this chapter. With them it carries light. If we try to put it in place of them, it becomes less than Christian.

The New Testament tells us that what we most truly need is to love and be loved. If we do not love, life can become as agonizing as for the woman who committed suicide and left the note, "I am killing myself because I have never sincerely loved any human being in all my life." If we are not loved, no other gifts can replace the one thing missing. Clinical histories are full of case studies of crushed personalities of children in privileged homes, given every advantage of life except genuine parental love. Giving or receiving, "the gift without the giver is bare."

In earth's highways and byways the Golden Rule means many things. In the gospel it means, "Love your neighbor as yourself."

13 : TRUE AND FALSE FAITH

From the Sermon on the Mount read Matthew 7:13-20.
For the parallel passages see Luke 6:43-45; 13:24.
To follow up the theme look at Matthew 12:33-35; Galatians 5:22-23; James 2:14-26.

❦ ONE OF THE greatest of virtues, as our society sees it, is to be broad-minded. We encourage a general goodwill, on the assumption that most people, whatever their mistakes, are headed in the right direction. To doubt this is to be intolerant.

At this point Jesus meets us with a quite different teaching. "Enter by the narrow gate; for the gate is wide and the way is easy, that leads to destruction, and those who enter by it are many. For the gate is narrow and the way is hard, that leads to life, and those who find it are few" (Matt. 7:13-14).

The Narrow Gate

Here we must be unusually careful to understand what Jesus means. If we remember his command against judging others, we will never boast that we are saved while many are heading for destruction. If we remember the place of love in his gospel, we will never scorn those who are not going our way. Too many Christians across the ages have read these verses with a satisfied feeling and a happy prayer, "God, I thank thee that I am not like other men" (Luke 18:11).

With these warnings burning in our minds we must still ask what Jesus means by the narrow gate and the difficult way. We may find that the answer has painful force for our time.

The twentieth century has been an age of the testing of faith. Great forces have risen to shake men's loyalties. We see this clearly in the case of the new faiths that have stirred revolutions, sent armies trampling across nations, and changed the maps of the world. Make no mistake: the modern movements of Nazism and Soviet Communism are, in their way, religions. They have their creeds, their heresies, their acts of worship, their reliance upon powers beyond anything human, their prophets and messiahs, their demands for faithfulness unto death, and their promises of salvation. Our major wars have not been over such issues as the fixing of national boundaries or the inheritance of the right to a throne. They have been ideological wars. They have marked clashes between "ways of life," outlooks upon mankind and the universe, basic faiths. Political leaders have called nations to show loyalty to their convictions, to put into action their creeds. The point comes when one must say in dead earnest: If Jesus Christ is right, contradictory faiths are wrong.

All this we can see fairly clearly. We can sympathize with people living under the sway of destructive ideologies. We can understand how, for them, the way to destruction is broad and easy. We honor the heroes and martyrs who refuse to go with the throngs.

But the problem goes far deeper and comes closer to home. It is not just a question of the place one lives and the government that asks loyalty. It is a question of the warring faiths and impulses within every personality. People who proclaim their loyalty to the church and utterly despise "materialistic communism" may be quite materialistic in their competition for wealth. Every honest Christian must admit that a thousand temptations draw him away from the kingdom of God. Jesus speaks directly to his own church when he says: "The gate is narrow and the way is hard, that leads to life."

Of course, we prefer a more comfortable religion. A popular book published in the rosier days of 1925 said that the God of Jesus was "not a stern Judge . . . but a kindly indulgent, joy-loving Father." Jesus, it said, "was notably tolerant of almost all kinds of sinners."

That reduces the message of divine mercy to a cheap piece of wishful thinking. Yes, God's love is infinite, and in his compassion he never ceases to seek the lost sheep. But some sheep, including some who love to proclaim that they are saved, keep running away. They reject that free grace which would transform their lives. They want no part of that "blessedness" described in the Beatitudes.

Why shouldn't the way be hard? Men will discipline themselves, adjusting their living habits and directing their ambitions for years, to make a football team or play the violin. Can the deepest concerns of life require less?

Even when we understand Jesus' words, we may distort his message. These last few paragraphs have come perilously close. Our tendency is to look around us and say: How few of us have found the narrow gate to life; how many of them have found the wide gate to destruction! No. Jesus is not inviting us to survey the world and contemplate how many skeptics or Communists are doomed. It's a neat, easily learned psychological trick to shift the question from ourselves to others. He tells us the way is hard, and we think he means it is hard for somebody else. He says, "I am the way" (John 14:6); and we avoid the challenge by saying, "What about all those other people?" He sees our dodge, and tells us (as he told Peter when Peter started worrying about John): What is that to you? You follow me. (See John 21:15-23.)

"By Their Fruits"

Jesus predicted accurately that there would be false prophets. His phrase, "a wolf in sheep's clothing," has become proverbial. Anyone can learn a pretty speech and promise us entrance to heaven, or a miracle in government, or a transformed personality.

The early church faced the problem. In its days of great missionary expansion there were many traveling prophets and evangelists. Some mixed their own vanity with their mission, and lured men into various heresies. Some others, with no allegiance to Jesus, found such a career an easy way to a meal ticket and a home wherever they went. The church had to learn to sift out the impostors. It went back to the words, "You will know them by their fruits."

This was a practical test. Do they come with acts of helpfulness, or with grasping hands? Do they encourage deeper fellowship, or do they stir up dissension?

That kind of test appeals to us practical Americans. No elaborate theories. Just a look at the fruit. A popular American philosophy is called pragmatism. The word looks, and means, something like practicalism. Pragmatists hold that the practical course of action is best; they choose the plan that works. There's just one gap in their theory as it is often expounded. Yes, we want the plan that works. But *for what goal* does it work? Often that question is left unanswered. Jesus offers a pragmatic test, but the testing takes place within the Christian faith. He tells us to look for the fruits—fruits that resemble the ways of the kingdom of God.

All through the Sermon on the Mount, Jesus has been pushing our thought back behind actions to motivations. Now he tells us that motivations bear fruit in actions.

Earlier he said that there was no virtue in an outward act that did not grow out of an inner sincerity. Now he fills out the picture by saying that inner sincerity will produce visible acts. The fundamental thing is the faith, hope, and love that set the character and direction of life. But these express themselves in all that we do.

The church has often argued about the relative importance of faith and works. Some of the arguments could easily have been solved by looking at Jesus' message. The arguments become unrealistic when they separate faith from works. Jesus is saying that the two go together. The inward is primary; the outward follows.

When we understand that, we see easily that works *without faith* are empty and that *faith without works is dead*. Each of these ideas is worth attention.

Works Without Faith Are Empty

A practical age like our own is likely to say that only actions count. We've often heard it said, "I'm not interested in your beliefs; I only want to know whether you can deliver the goods."

Of course no one really believes that. Suppose a Communist, who is actually loyal to Russia rather than the United States, is discovered in a key governmental position. No one says, "It doesn't matter, so long as he has committed no crimes." We recognize immediately that *loyalty* (which is akin to faith) is more basic than any isolated act.

Likewise, in the international negotiations of recent times, we have heard repeatedly the phrase, "good faith." If we could count on good faith, many other worries would settle them-selves. But neither promises nor acts make us feel secure if we doubt that there is good faith.

Clearly, then, works cannot take the place of faith. Jesus' most scathing denunciations went to men who did numerous good things, but whose deeds were expressions of their own pride or efforts to win the approval of God. Jesus probed beneath the acts to the faith that prompted them.

There is a second reason why acts alone are empty. Recall some of the qualities of the blessed man, according to Jesus' definition. He is poor in spirit, merciful, sympathetic, thirsty for righteousness, pure in heart, loving, forgiving, sincere, trust-ing. These are not qualities that we can drum up inside our-selves. As we have seen before, no one can claim such spiritual accomplishment as to earn a place in God's kingdom. Rather, a loving and forgiving God offers us a place in his kingdom. Our response to God's mercy is *faith*. In that faith we enter into the spirit of his kingdom. Not by earnest effort, but by trusting him do we approach him. Once the *trust* (another word which is close to faith) is there, we can do some striving.

Faith Without Works Is Dead

If good works truly are the expression of faith, then true faith expresses itself in helpfulness. It has its fruits. The New Testa-ment letter of James resoundingly asserts: "Faith without works is dead." We could just as well say that faith without works is not really faith. The phrase *faith without works*, as Augustine suggests, is like the phrase, "warm snow." There is no such thing. When snow becomes warm, it ceases to be snow. When faith bears no fruits, it is not really faith.

During a dramatic evangelistic campaign some time ago, someone noticed a passenger on a bus, talking to the driver in obviously intense enthusiasm. As the driver slowed the bus for the next stop, the passenger's voice was heard: "Oh, don't stop for them niggers. I just got saved, and I've got to get home as soon as I can to tell my wife about it!"

We have a right to wonder about that kind of salvation. With Jesus' warning in our ears, we know that we cannot comprehend the degree of sincerity in the convert's heart, nor assert that he is inferior to ourselves. But we can say that his "salvation" does not comprehend the "blessedness" of the Sermon on the Mount.

The Protestant Christian tradition has emphasized the theme of "justification by faith" rather than by works. (Justification means entering into a right relationship with God.) The apostle Paul gave us the phrase, and Martin Luther rediscovered it. But both insisted that faith finds expression in works.

In the letter where, above all others, Paul emphasized faith rather than works and the Spirit rather than the Law, he wrote that the "fruit of the Spirit is love, joy, peace, patience, kindness, goodness, faithfulness, gentleness, self-control." (See Galatians 5:22-23.) And in his argument for faith as against the Roman Catholic law, Luther used Jesus' figure of the tree and its fruit. Faith, he said, forms the roots; they nourish the fruits (the good works). And this is the way Jesus puts it. (See Matthew 12:33-35 and Luke 6:43-45.)

14 : WORSHIP AND WORK

From the Sermon on the Mount read Matthew 7:21-23.
For the parallel passages see Luke 6:46; 13:25-30.
To follow up the theme look at Matthew 12:46-50; 21:28-31; 25:31-46.

THE WORLD has tried to get rid of Jesus in two ways, someone has said. The first was to crucify him. That failed. The risen Lord could win more people than the man of Nazareth. The second way was to worship him. That has almost worked.

But how can it almost work? How can people get rid of him by worshiping him? Will not every thought of Jesus, every bit of devotion toward him, draw us closer to him?

No. Not necessarily. The ways of the human personality are subtle and devious. The mind knows a thousand tricks to dodge an issue.

It takes a certain amount of bravado to stand up and defy God. That is occasionally done, usually by people trying to attract attention. But the more common device, which takes no nerve at all, is to adapt God to our petty thoughts and desires. We can do this without ever letting on to our closest friends or to ourselves that we are doing it.

Hence that disturbing Dane, Sören Kierkegaard, could say: "The Christianity of the New Testament simply does not exist." Instead, millions of people through the centuries have cunningly "sought little by little to cheat God out of Christianity, and have succeeded in making Christianity exactly the opposite of what it is in the New Testament."[1]

Does Kierkegaard exaggerate? Certainly we hope so. But as we have studied the Sermon on the Mount, we must frequently have had an uneasy feeling that led us to a judgment something like Kierkegaard's.

The Problem in the New Testament

The process started early. In the short ministry of Jesus it got under way. With his typical directness—some would call it tactlessness—he met it head on.

Look at the record in the Bible. There, in the next to last paragraph of the Sermon on the Mount, is the unmistakable warning: It is not enough to say, "Lord, Lord." The need is to

---

[1] *Attack upon Christendom* by Sören Kierkegaard, translated by Walter Lowrie, pp. 32-33. Princeton University Press, 1944. Used by permission.

do the will of the heavenly Father. Luke's version is still more
direct and poignant than Matthew's: "Why do you call me
Lord and not do what I tell you?" (Luke 6:46)

The next two sentences (in Matthew) carry us in imagination
to the Day of Judgment. (Compare them with the more detailed
parable of judgment in Matthew 25:31-46.) Once again we see
that the Sermon on the Mount is not merely moral advice. It is
the Good News of God's kingdom for those who accept it, and
the fateful news of doom for those who reject it. We see the
vivid picture of despairing, painful response from Jesus, "I never
knew you," and the command (quoted from Psalm 6:8), "De-
part from me, all you workers of evil."

The words are still alive today. We think of the Easter throngs
crowding the churches to sing, "Christ the Lord is ris'n today"—
many of them there merely because church is the place prescribed by American folkways for the display of spring finery.
We think of ornate church buildings where people go to forget
their troubles—and to hear sermons which never remind them
of the slums in the shadow of the sanctuary. We think of uneasy folk engaged in the "return to religion" because they yearn
for "peace of mind"—never realizing that Jesus grants peace only
to those who follow him along the path of lowly service. As
vividly as did Jesus himself, we hear the words, "Lord, Lord,"
and see the refusal to do the will of God. We too are guilty.

The Perils of Worship

The life without reverence is barren and insensitive. And worship is the proper expression of reverence. The Sermon on the
Mount leads to adoration, thanksgiving, and prayer as truly as it
leads to acts of service. But there are perils in worship.

Some of the worship that goes on in our churches is merely
lip service, talk takes the place of activity. True worship is the
expression of the reverence of a human personality for his Lord
and Creator. Reverence makes us eager to serve and obey. But
false worship and lip service can be worse then open defiance.

The story is told of Mark Twain's encounter with a man who managed to combine the appearances of piety with a predatory career in business. "Before I die," said the hypocrite, "I mean to make a pilgrimage to the Holy Land. I will climb to the top of Mount Sinai and read the Ten Commandments aloud." "I have a better idea," answered Mark Twain. "Why don't you stay right at home in Boston and keep them?"

After the warmth of the worship that says, "Lord, Lord," there is a chill in the words, "Do what I say." But if we do not meet the chill, the warmth is not the warmth of life. Bishop Gore ended his book, *The Sermon on the Mount,* by saying: "Many will come to him in that day with a record of their orthodoxy and of their observances, of their brilliant successes in his professed service; but he will protest unto them, 'I never knew you.' He 'knows' no man in whom he cannot recognize his own likeness."[2]

His own likeness? If we understand the Sermon on the Mount, we will never claim that. But if it sinks in, it does begin to remake us.

Doing God's Will: Evangelism

What happens when we take seriously the Christian opportunity and responsibility to do the will of God and the things that Jesus taught? Probably it means more than we usually think. God asks of us a whole life. He is not satisfied with a few externals that do not touch the heart. Nor does he want some religious emotionalism that generates no activity.

This seems obvious. Yet church people misunderstand it every day. To accept the Sermon on the Mount will require some changes in several areas of our Christian living.

One of these areas is evangelism. The word is what the experts call a "loaded" word. It carries an emotional load beyond its

---

[2] *The Sermon on the Mount* by Charles Gore, p. 188. John Murray Ltd., London.

literal meaning; it obscures our thinking because we respond favorably or unfavorably to its sound, before we think what it means.

Two common meanings of the word are mistaken. (1) Some church literature gives the impression that evangelism is identical with increasing the number of names on the church rolls. This meaning is obviously too shallow. Of course, the follower of Christ belongs in the fellowship of followers. But, as Jesus keeps insisting, you can take part in the organization and never really meet God. Perhaps the biggest evangelistic job today is *within* the churches.

(2) Some people think of evangelism as a campaign that stirs up an emotional turmoil and produces a dramatic experience of being "saved." Let's not deny that some people can come to God in that way. But such an experience may leave a person as far as his pagan neighbors from the Sermon on the Mount. In some religion, as Phillips Brooks said, the boiler has no connection with the engine. The words, "Lord, Lord," are there. The service of God throughout the whole of life is absent.

When we understand what evangelism is, we recognize it as the responsibility of every Christian. Evangelism is the carrying of the gospel to men. It is no job to be left to the professionals. It is one of the things Jesus bade us do. If we say, "Lord, Lord," but do nothing to help others find his gift and know his will, we may expect to hear that he does not know us.

Stewardship and Vocation

If we do the things Jesus tells us, we make all of life a part of his service. We recognize ourselves as God's stewards. Life and all its benefits are God's gifts, entrusted to us for a time. In the earning of our daily bread we are conscious of a calling to serve our fellowmen. In the use of our abilities and our wealth, we can honor God and do his will. The purpose of life becomes, in the phrase of the Calvinists, "to glorify God and enjoy him forever."

Yet how seldom does it occur, even to faithful churchmen, to consider the new job offer, with its increased salary, in terms of religious opportunities? And how seldom do we think of spending or investing our incomes—apart from the fraction given to worthy causes—in terms of serving God?

A paper published by a religious agency in the Philippine Islands justifies gambling with the argument that "we are entitled to set aside a fair share of our money for entertainment, and if we think it is all right to spend that money on gambling, God doesn't care." Note how the argument avoids the whole issue of stewardship. But no more so than the common statement we often hear, "I earned the money, and I'm entitled to spend it as I please." The man who says that, though he might be a tither, is not a steward. Not that religion leaves no place for enjoyment. We can enjoy our work, our worship, our recreation. What we cannot do is divide life into segments, saying "Lord, Lord," in some activities and assuming that "God doesn't care" about the rest.

The Life of the Nations

We have seen that the Sermon on the Mount gives no direct advice about the activities of government. But we have seen, too, that it gives us no right to divide life between "religious" and "secular" spheres, saying "Lord, Lord" in one, and going our sinful way undisturbed in the other.

Therefore we cannot help asking why centuries of Christian worship have not made more difference in the life of the nations. The bitter but deeply troubled Thomas Hardy once wrote:

> "Peace upon earth!" was said, We sing it,
> And pay a million priests to bring it.
> After two thousand years of mass
> We've got as far as poison-gas.[3]

---

[3] From "Christmas: 1924" in Winter Words in Various Moods and Metres. The Macmillan Co., 1929. Used by permission.

The history of the twentieth century is a bitter one for us to acknowledge. It embarrasses our missionaries when the so-called heathen nations ask about the behavior of the so-called Christian nations. Granted, plenty of the misery of this century has been the work of men who were defiantly anti-Christian. But much of it came from men who worshiped but did not obey.

The sessions of the United States Congress regularly open with prayer. No doubt there would be protests if the chaplains ceased to say, "Lord, Lord." But there might be real cries of pain if the prayers made a difference in the national life. Powerful lobbies would interfere with the public interest less often. Nationalism would give way before the needs of this one world.

But this, say some, is politics and economics, not religion. As though Jesus had said, "Do the will of my Father—except in some areas of life." What is left for religion, says Lewis Mumford, if political and economic life are unaffected? "Little more than a brief code for mating, a ceremonial for marriage, chicken broth and visitation for the ill, and a few seemly words and gestures at the burial service."[4] What is left? Mainly the chance to say, "Lord, Lord."

15 : THE VOICE WITH AUTHORITY

From the Sermon on the Mount read Matthew 7:24-29.
For the parallel passage see Luke 6:47-49.
To follow up the theme look at 1 Corinthians 3:10-15.

ON DANIEL WEBSTER'S tomb in Marshfield, Massachusetts, is the epitaph which the famous statesman dictated the day before his death:

[4] *Faith for Living* by Lewis Mumford, p. 152. Harcourt, Brace & World, Inc., 1940. Used by permission.

"Philosophical argument . . . has sometimes shaken my reason for the faith which is in me; but my heart has always assured and reassured me that the gospel of Jesus Christ must be Divine Reality. The Sermon on the Mount cannot be a mere human production. This belief enters into the very depth of my conscience. The whole history of man proves it."

According to Matthew, those who first heard Jesus had a similar reaction. Without benefit of all the centuries of history that Webster looked at, they sensed something amazing. "The crowds were astonished at his teaching, for he taught them as one who had authority, and not as their scribes."

A New Authority

Even on the surface the note of authority was obvious. Jesus' listeners were acquainted with two kinds of appeal to authority in their tradition. First, they knew the scribes, who started from the authority of the Mosaic Law, then expounded it. Second, they knew the inspired prophets, who started with the ringing declaration, "Thus says the Lord." But Jesus did neither. We have seen how he introduced startling statements with the words, "but I say to you." We have seen how he looked ahead to the day of judgment when some will hear him say, "I never knew you." No wonder people said he spoke with authority.

There had been other clues along the way. At the synagogue in Capernaum people were astonished, "for he taught them as one who had authority." Immediately afterwards, when he healed a sick man, spectators marveled that he had authority even over unclean spirits. (See Mark 1:22, 27 and Luke 4:32, 36.) Still more amazing—some thought it blasphemous—was his assumption of authority to forgive sins (Matthew 9:2-8).

All these signs led to the recognition on a deeper level that there was some mysterious power and authority in Jesus himself. But, before we can understand that, we need to consider what we mean by authority.

Three Kinds of Authority

1. Often when we speak of authority we mean some pro-nouncement that settles an issue for us. This authority is ex-ternal. The parent *decides* some issues for the child—wisely, we hope, but whether wisely or not, the decision is made. Congress *decides* the rates for income taxes; we citizens have some influence on the decision, but whether we like it or not, we acknowledge its authority. Such external authorities can change their minds. When they do, we are bound by the new decision rather than the old.

Such authority may exist in religion. The Pharisees accepted the authority of a code of laws and its official interpretation. Our Roman Catholic friends accept the authority of the pope. When he changes his mind, as he has often done, they change accordingly—whether it be a question of belief or of the rules for fasting. Although they may voluntarily accept the authority, it is external to themselves.

2. Sometimes people who chafe under authority rebel and say: "I am tired of having someone decide things for me. I reject authority. From now on, I'll make my own decisions. I recognize no authority except myself." Usually this kind of protest is quite impractical, but it may give one a tremendous feeling of exhilaration, at least temporarily.

Unfortunately, people often seem to think there are only these two kinds of authority. They think: Either I am the master of my soul, or I am the slave of someone else. Either I am my own authority, or I submit to some external authority.

But there is a third kind of authority.

3. Truth is an authority that no one can long defy. It is superior to any individual; yet it is not external to us. It is im-bedded in ourselves and our universe. It does not change its mind and then require us to change accordingly. Unless we are hopelessly adolescent rebels, we know we must come to terms with truth.

God is that kind of authority. Because he made us in his image, something of his truth is part of our inmost beings. When we defy him, we defy our truest selves. When we respond to his Word, we say: "This is no alien voice, no external commander ordering me around. Nor is it any mere whim of my own. This is no ruler who may change his mind tomorrow. This is my Creator. He calls me to be true to that self which he made and filled with the breath of life, not to this twisted self that is torn by conflicting loyalties and warped understanding. This is the authority of the Physician who can heal, the Savior who can redeem, the Creator who can even now give new life."

That is why Christian faith has always said we are most truly ourselves, not when we boast of our independence but when we love; not when we command but when we serve; not when we buck the truth but when we freely accept what is given.

That is why we recognize that Christ speaks with authority.

The Sermon and the Christian Gospel

The authority of the Sermon on the Mount is like the authority of the rock foundation in that final striking parable. In the debris of history are countless crumbled buildings, shattered when their sand foundations washed away. This rock foundation endures. It is the Rock of Ages, the Rock of Eternity.

But the truth of the Sermon is not just abstract truth, locked in sentences which we tediously translate and study. You can lose or misunderstand a sentence here or there, and the truth remains. For it is the truth of the living Spirit who gave us the sentences, the truth of the God who acted through this man teaching on the mount for our salvation.

Martin Dibelius points out that many of the sentences of Jesus have parallels in the sayings of Jewish literature. Yet the rabbinic statements won no authority outside Judaism. Why did the Sermon on the Mount inspire such universal acclaim? Because it was Jesus who proclaimed these sayings.

Occasionally you may have heard the curious idea that the Sermon on the Mount is a simple moral message, which has nothing to do with the rest of the church's teaching about Jesus. Someone says: "I don't believe all this theology, but I believe in the simple teachings of Jesus."

But you cannot say that, if you know what is in the Sermon on the Mount. A vast, profound theology is there. There is the promise of God's kingdom, the assurance that man can trust God, the warning that we are evil, an ethic so searching that it convicts us of sin and sends us helplessly searching for life, the prayer for forgiveness, the confidence that a merciful God will forgive, the warning that life stands under divine judgment and that the voice that speaks the sermon will be the voice heard at the judgment. All this is in the Sermon.

Still the Sermon is not the entire Christian gospel. It makes us ready to hear the gospel. As Archibald Hunter says, "If God means that, in order to be saved, we must completely fulfill all these demands, then we are all doomed to be damned."[1] But the gospel goes on to tell us that this Jesus, who gave us the Sermon, was crucified, that in his very crucifixion he forgave his murderers, that his forgiveness was the forgiveness of God for humankind. It goes on to say that God raised from the dead this Jesus, the Lord and Savior of all who trust him.

That is the only reason we have the Sermon on the Mount. Otherwise it would have been lost long ago. But the early Christians were convinced that in this Jesus, the eternal God had entered into human life for the salvation of men. This "gospel" —the word, you remember, means "good news"—was the most tremendous thing in their lives. So they collected and treasured the words which Jesus spoke when he was on earth, passed them on to newcomers in their fellowship, and wrote them down in the "Gospels" that are now part of our New Testament. These were the sayings of their Lord who reigned in heaven, the Savior

---

[1] *A Pattern for Life* by Archibald Hunter, p. 102. The Westminster Press, 1953. Used by permission.

who had bestowed upon them the Holy Spirit, who had promised and brought into their midst the revolutionary power of the kingdom of God.

Building on Rock

The Sermon on the Mount ends with the parable of the two houses. "How terrifyingly it is driven home!" said Augustine. Look at some of the phrases. "These words of mine"—there's the note of authority we have seen. Everyone who "does them" and who "does not do them"—that is absolutely clear and leaves us no out. Then the two men—one building on rock, the other on sand. The listeners perhaps thought of the desert wadies, streams that are dry most of the year. The smooth sand might seem an inviting place to build, and in calm days the house would seem secure. But then come rain, flood, and wind—like the struggles which come into every life. One house stands; the other falls.

It's clear, but still puzzling. Can we really build a life upon this foundation that Christ offers? We have seen in our study many ways of dodging the issue. Let them pass in review. One method is to reduce the whole thing to some practical version of the Golden Rule, or to identify it with the common goals of Americanism. That can be done only in ignorance or dishonesty. The opposite method is to make it all an ideal, not quite practical but lovely to aspire to. That is certainly not making it the foundation rock. In between these two are the many variations on them. Some say this kind of life is possible within a Christian community, but not among outsiders. Some reserve many of Jesus' "counsels" for the lives of a few saints, and frankly settle for a good deal less everywhere else.

Jesus does not allow these evasions. True, he is proclaiming the kingdom of God in all its holiness and purity. We can say in complete truthfulness that the kingdoms of this world are still far, far from the kingdom of God. And we must live in the kingdoms of this world. But Jesus calls on us to seek God's kingdom. So what shall we do with this disturbing preacher?

One qualification we have discussed. Jesus was not legislating for any conceivable civil government. If in democratic citizenship we take responsibility for government, we cannot rush the Sermon on the Mount through Congress. Governments provide for laws, courts, powers of enforcement, the maintenance of objective norms of overt actions—things which the Sermon on the Mount dismisses. Yet even in this area of government we cannot ignore Jesus.

"You can do anything with bayonets except sit on them," said Bismarck. Coercion and armies do things—we cannot escape it. But they are not the rock foundation on which a house can sit through wind and flood.

What, then, of our personal lives—insofar as we can distinguish them from political life? No one has such trust in God, such disdain for mammon, such courage and faithfulness that he can claim to have built on rock. Much of what we have built —what every one of us has built—is doomed to crash. Many of our dearest accomplishments are destined for destruction "on that day" of which Jesus speaks.

If we recognize that, the Sermon has done something for us. "It plants a seed of permanent dissatisfaction in the soul,"[2] says Amos Wilder. It sends us to the Father, with whom there is forgiveness.

But that forgiveness, if sincerely received, is no idle escape hatch. It is the source of the trust and confidence which alone can—with some reality in every Christian life—bring alive in humanity the spirit that Jesus demands and imparts.

"Thy kingdom come," the Sermon teaches us to pray. That kingdom comes with storm and destruction to our works of proud ambition. It comes with healing mercy to the merciful who trust in God and long for the "blessedness" that he offers.

A fitting conclusion for a study of the Sermon on the Mount is a prayer from the Book of Common Order:

---

[2] The Interpreter's Bible, Vol. VII, p. 155. Abingdon Press, 1951.

Give ear, O Lord, unto our prayer, and attend to the voice of our supplication.

Make us poor in spirit: that ours may be the kingdom of heaven.

Make us to mourn for sin: that we may be comforted by thy grace.

Make us to hunger and thirst after righteousness: that we may be filled therewith.

Make us merciful: that we may obtain mercy.

Make us pure in heart: that we may see thee.

Make us peacemakers: that we may be called thy children.

Make us willing to be persecuted for righteousness' sake: that our reward may be great in heaven. Amen.

A STUDY GUIDE

If this book is used in study groups, the questions below may be useful. Some can be answered by studying the biblical materials. Others call for thinking and an exchange of opinions within the group. Many of them do not have a "correct" answer that has been determined in advance.

CHAPTER 1

The questions deal with every chapter except the first, which is an introductory discussion not based on a specific text from the Sermon on the Mount.

CHAPTER 2

1. If (without mentioning religion) you were to ask a dozen people what gives them most happiness, what answers would

you expect? How do these answers compare with Jesus' conception?

2. Is Mark Twain right about our difficulty with the Bible? Give evidence.

3. Is it true that "Jesus is more radical than the most radical of our political revolutionaries"? Note that the word radical, like radish comes from the Latin word for root.

4. Someone has said: "If Christians knew what they were saying when they pray, 'thy kingdom come, thy will be done,' they would quake in their boots every time they 'repeat the Lord's Prayer.'" Do you agree? Why, or why not?

5. Look up Revelation 3:17 and relate it to the lesson.

6. How well does the Gilbert and Sullivan advice actually work?

7. Would anyone today make the second-century criticism of Christianity, quoted above? Should we be glad or sorry? Why?

8. Do the persecuted people who produced the Negro spirituals represent the poor in spirit who find the kingdom of heaven? What of the Pentecostal sects in our city slums? Who are the poor in spirit today, and why does the church so often fail them?

9. "Unless you turn and become like children, you will never enter the kingdom of heaven" (Matt. 18:3). What do you suppose Jesus means? What is Christian maturity, and what has it to do with becoming like little children?

CHAPTER 3

1. Tolstoi, the Russian novelist and philosopher, once noted how people are inclined to regard "their own so-called civilization as the true civilization." Some of the standards of the "civilized man," as he observed them, included: "finishing one's studies, keeping one's nails clean, using the tailor's and the barber's services, traveling abroad." What are the comparable standards by which people are respected in your community? Is real worth sometimes overlooked because of these standards?

How do they compare with Jesus' standards? Consult the standard in 1 Samuel 16:7.

2. Give an example of a situation in which you admire laughter more than grief, and one in which you admire grief more than laughter.

3. In your community what are some of the things that people crave? Are people satisfied?

4. According to Jesus, what prevents us from seeing God? What about honest doubt? How can we distinguish honest doubt from the doubt that is a cover-up for unwillingness to face God? (See if Matthew 11:25 offers any help.)

5. Is the bully usually a man with real strength? Or is he covering up his weakness?

6. What are some opportunities you have for showing mercy and for making peace?

7. Prepare a set of modern "Beatitudes" that typify the spirit of our culture. For instance, "Blessed are the go-getters, for they will succeed," or "Blessed are the wealthy, for they will find honor and comfort." Compare them with the Beatitudes of Jesus.

CHAPTER 4

1. What groups in American life seem most willing to undergo persecution for their beliefs? Can we discover why they are so willing?

2. What is the meaning of the description of the church of Laodicea in Revelation 3:14-16? Is this a fair description of the American church? Give evidence.

3. "Be faithful unto death, and I will give you the crown of life" (Rev. 2:10). What does this statement mean to us?

4. In the early church it was said: "The blood of martyrs is the seed of the church." What does this mean for the church today, both in other lands and in America?

5. What is the martyr-complex? How is it related to Jesus' teaching?

6. One modern writer has described Jesus as "the most popular dinner guest in Jerusalem." On the basis of your study of all the Beatitudes, how truthful do you think this description is?

7. In the lesson from Luke, Jesus says: "Woe to you, when all men speak well of you, for so their fathers did to the false prophets." Does anybody believe this today? Why does Jesus consider popularity so dangerous? Is it a dangerous temptation for us?

8. What are some of the costs of discipleship today? In what areas is the church unwilling to pay the cost?

9. Have you ever been a cowardly Christian?

10. A hymn, popular among many young people's groups, has Christ ask whether his followers are able to be crucified with him. The answer is sung, "Lord, we are able." One youth group had been using the hymn as a frequent favorite. One night they got to discussing its meaning. They decided it was glib for a group, which was facing no major inconvenience (to say nothing of persecution) for its faith, to sing: Lord we are able—to be crucified. The result was that they stopped using the hymn. Were they right?

CHAPTER 5

1. You can probably recall many times when Americans, paying taxes to help support foreign aid programs, have complained, saying, "But those people aren't even grateful; they don't even give us credit for helping them." Consider that attitude in terms of Christ's teaching about good deeds. If foreign aid is given for political reasons, would we be wiser to say so candidly rather than pretending to act out of generosity?

2. Evaluate the statement quoted from Charles Lamb.

3. Is the example of the church building fund typical or unusual?

4. A Christian minister once spent several months working in a factory. Afterwards one of the workers commented: "He was just one of us. No one knew at the time that he was a

preacher." Should the minister have been gratified or disappointed at this statement? Consider carefully the pros and cons of the question.

5. How much do your fellow workers throughout the week know about your religious life? Are you satisfied with your answer?

6. Some Christians wear a small cross or other symbol of churchmanship. Is this a good idea? Why is it often easier to wear an emblem of a Masonic order, the American Legion, or a political party?

7. Semantics (the study of the precise meaning and flavor of words) has become a popular subject. Analyze the effect of these terms: Holier-than-thou, pharisaical, puritanical, sanctimonious, willing to take a stand, secretive, forthright.

8. Think of some situation in which social pressures are tempting you to unchristian behavior. Consider the possible responses:

(a) Yielding to the pressure. (Refusing to let your light shine.)

(b) Declaring your virtue. (Doing good, to be seen of men.)

Is there a way of expressing Christian convictions without self-righteousness?

CHAPTER 6

1. A common phrase in our conversation is, "He means well." On what occasions do we use that phrase? Someone has said that it is one of the cruelest things that can be said about a person. Why? In the light of the New Testament how might we evaluate it?

2. Immanuel Kant said: "There is nothing good without qualification except a good will." What do you think he meant?

3. Paul said: "If I deliver my body to be burned, but have not love, I gain nothing" (1 Cor. 13:3). Why? Could a person really make such a sacrifice without genuine love and devotion?

4. Restate Matthew 5:23-24 so as to bring it up to date.

5. Martin Luther, in his enthusiasm for the "inward" character of the gospel, said: "If we had enough of the Holy Spirit, we could write new Ten Commandments clearer than those which came from Moses." Do you agree? Do you think it is safe to try? Why?

6. When Luther wrote his own catechism, he used the Ten Commandments from the Bible, not his own. Why do you think he made this decision?

7. James Whitcomb Riley said:

> The meanest man I ever saw
> Allus kep' inside o' the law.

Can you relate that saying to the Sermon on the Mount?

8. In his acts and teachings Jesus criticized the religion of legalism, yet insisted that God's demands were rigorous. Can you give examples from life today of situations (a) where the church is too legalistic and (b) where the church does not present God's demands in their severity.

CHAPTER 7

1. Can you point to cases where people have followed the ethic of Jesus referred to in this chapter? What was the result?

2. We sometimes call people generous because they treat their friends nicely. What does Matthew 5:46 have to say of this?

3. Should congregational prayers ask God's blessing on Russia and Communist China? Would your community favor such prayers? Your church?

4. Is it possible to coerce others without hatred? As examples consider a parent and child, a policeman and a law violator, a nation and its enemies.

5. Tennyson, looking at the cruelty in human history, including religious wars and persecutions, wrote:

> Love your enemy, bless your haters, said the
> Greatest of the great;

> Christian love among the churches look'd the
> twin of heathen hate.

Is this statement just? What does it mean for the Christian church?

6. Winston Churchill in *The Gathering Storm* wrote:

"Those who are . . . ready to fight whenever some challenge comes from a foreign power, have not always been right. . . . How many wars have been averted by patience and persisting goodwill! Religion and virtue alike lend their sanctions to meekness and humility, not only between men but between nations.

"The Sermon on the Mount is the last word in Christian ethics. Everyone respects the Quakers. Still, it is not on these terms that ministers assume their responsibility of guiding states. . . . The safety of the state, the lives and freedom of their own fellow countrymen, to whom they owe their position, make it right and imperative in the last resort, or when a final and definite conviction has been reached, that the use of force should not be excluded."[1]

Discuss each paragraph of this statement separately, asking whether Churchill is right. Compare his statement with that of the American president in chapter 3, page 20.

CHAPTER 8

1. What do you think are the real motives for prayer?

2. Dietrich Bonhoeffer, a great Christian leader, was executed by the Nazis. From his solitary confinement in prison, he wrote to his parents: "I am not so unused to solitude as some people would be, and it is quite as good as a turkish bath for the soul." How does this statement reflect Jesus' teaching?

3. What values are there in solitary prayer? In the common

---

[1] *The Gathering Storm* by Winston Churchill, p. 320. Houghton Mifflin Co., 1948. Used by permission.

prayer of a community of believers? Are there dangers in either mode of prayer if it is used exclusively?

4. What are some common ways of violating the prayer, "Hallowed be thy name"? What of irreverent language? What of attempts to "use" God in selfish prayers or in controversies?

5. What specific phrases in the Lord's Prayer are made more clear by preceding portions of the Sermon on the Mount?

6. One can assemble from prayers of Judaism a composite prayer which, though much more elaborate than the Lord's Prayer, includes parallels to each sentence in the latter. What would you say is the originality of the Lord's Prayer? Is it the brevity and literary style? Is it the unique meaning that Jesus gave to old words like Father, thy kingdom, thy will? Is it the meaning that he gave the prayer by his own life?

CHAPTER 9

1. Do you think the story of the unbaptized right arms applies to churchmen today? If so, can you give some typical examples (of attitudes and activities, not of persons)?

2. The God of Israel was called a "jealous" God. What does the word mean in terms of Jesus' teaching?

3. Why does American civilization seem to be more obsessed with wealth than many other civilizations?

4. In what sense is Christianity a "materialistic" religion?

5. How does the example of the proposed "Ideological War Council" fit the scripture for this chapter?

6. How fundamental do you think the "profit motive" is in American life? How often do people put love ahead of profit?

7. Can one pursue "treasures on earth" without losing his heart to them? Explain.

8. Give examples of situations in which we try to serve both God and mammon in (a) political life; (b) church life; (c) personal life.

9. Examine a popular magazine (such as Reader's Digest), a

group of comic strips, and some radio or TV programs. Find evidence as to how Americans are making the choice between God and mammon.

CHAPTER 10

1. The paragraph on young people in the chapter is based upon several studies, some made by young people. Is it a fair one?

2. How does the quotation from Marx and Engels throw light on the Communist attitude toward religion?

3. Why are people more anxious today than in many past generations?

4. The Gallup poll in 1952 asked the question: "What would you say is your biggest worry these days—the thing that disturbs you most?" Answers: Finances, 45 per cent; war or threat of war, 21 per cent; health problems, 17 per cent; job or business security, 4 per cent; miscellaneous, 8 per cent; no worries, 5 per cent. How might Christian faith affect these worries?

5. Try your own "Gallup poll" to see how much the situation has changed over the past several years.

6. Another survey showed that most people thought they needed about one-third more money for happiness—whether their income was large or small. How does this relate to our scripture?

7. The famous Swiss psychotherapist, C. G. Jung, was not a follower of any organized religion, and he had some biting things to say about the churches. But in a clinical practice dealing with "people from all the civilized countries of the earth" he found: "Among all my patients in the second half of life— that is to say, over thirty-five—there has not been one whose problem in the last resort was not that of finding a religious outlook on life. It is safe to say that every one of them fell ill because he had lost that which the living religions of every age

have given to their followers, and none of them has been really healed who did not regain his religious outlook."[2]

CHAPTER 11

1. What are some common reasons why we often misjudge people?

2. Is it possible to judge a deed without judging the doer? Or to pronounce an act wrong and yet sympathize with the person who did it?

3. You get a letter saying: "——— has applied for employment with us and has given your name as a reference. We wish to learn about his character, abilities, and personal qualities. Your reply will be considered confidential." Will the scripture for this chapter influence your reply? If so, how?

4. Are leniency and mercy the same? Explain.

5. Dwight Morrow, former American ambassador to Mexico, once commented on international relations: "We judge ourselves by our ideals; we judge others by their actions." Do you agree?

6. In C. S. Lewis' The Screwtape Letters a devil writes his nephew about a Christian whom the two want to mislead: "You must bring him to a condition in which he can practice self-examination for an hour without discovering any of those facts about himself which are perfectly clear to anyone who has ever lived in the same house with him or worked in the same office."[3] Is it really possible for anyone to get into such a situation?

7. Do we sometimes judge ourselves too severely? For example, some clinical case studies describe people who make elaborate self-examination of minute wrongs—all in order to avoid facing some really important problems in themselves. Does your experience agree?

---

[2] Modern Man in Search of a Soul by C. G. Jung, p. 264. Harcourt, Brace & World, Inc., 1933. Used by permission.

[3] The Screwtape Letters by C. S. Lewis, pp. 20-21. The Macmillan Co., 1943. Used by permission.

8. An American, talking to an Oriental, once said: "Has there ever been a nation so peace-loving, so generous, and so concerned with the sacredness of human life, as the United States?" Imagine yourself as the Oriental and work out the answer you would feel like making.

9. It is said that we typically use language in the following manner: I am firm, you are stubborn, he is pig-headed. I am shrewd, you are a sharp operator, he is a crook. Make your own examples.

CHAPTER 12

1. Were you ever in a situation like Huck Finn's, where your conscience bothered you no matter what you did?

2. Can a person *with good intentions* apply the Golden Rule in a harmful way? If so, how?

3. Why does the text say: "*The Golden Rule without the gospel can be a cheap standard of conduct*"? Do you agree?

4. "Do as you are done by." At just what point does this differ from the Golden Rule?

5. Dr. Fosdick advises a "Golden Rule in reverse: Whatsoever you would laugh at in others, laugh at in yourself." Why?

6. A newspaper quotes Dr. Buttrick as preaching that most people "mistakenly" believe that the Golden Rule "is the core of the Sermon on the Mount." Why mistakenly?

7. Does the Golden Rule offer a basis for agreement where other ethical and religious traditions divide men, as in the U. N.?

8. Did you ever know anyone who differed with the Golden Rule? How might such a person be persuaded to change his mind?

9. In France a few days after D-Day of the Second World War, three famous generals conferred—George Marshall, Dwight Eisenhower, and Omar Bradley. After they finished their business, they fell to talking about war and military leadership. We are told that they talked of great commanders since Gideon and

asked themselves, What is the indispensable quality for the leader who must order other men to face death?

The answer came in one word provided by General Marshall.

Decide what you think the answer should be. Then compare your answer with General Marshall's, which is given on page 112 below.

CHAPTER 13

1. Why is communism often considered a religion?

2. What aspects of American life make the way to destruction easy?

3. In Matthew, Jesus says that few find the way that leads to life. In Luke, someone asks him whether few will be saved. Notice how he answers (Luke 13:24). Why does he answer in just that way?

4. How does Jesus' advice about judging by fruits differ from American pragmatism?

5. Was Jesus' own life a success by the pragmatic test? Explain.

6. It is often said that actions speak louder than words. Do you agree? Do actions speak louder than faith?

7. Ralph Waldo Emerson said: "What you are . . . thunders so that I cannot hear what you say to the contrary." How does this apply to the subject of this chapter?

8. Evaluate these two statements: "It does not matter what a man believes so long as he behaves himself." "It does not matter whether a man loves his wife so long as he treats her well."

9. In every community there are some irreligious people who show more goodwill and helpfulness than the religious people. What does this mean?

CHAPTER 14

1. Evaluate the following statement: "The wholesale murder, torture, persecution, and oppression we are witnessing in

the middle of the twentieth century proves the complete bankruptcy of Christianity as a civilizing force."[4]

2. Examine the statement by Kierkegaard on the opening page of this chapter. How accurate is it?

3. "It is possible to be closer to God in seeking what God wills while denying his existence than in defending an unjust order of things while praising him."[5] Why do you think Bennett said this? Is he right?

4. "Worship is undoubtedly a bad thing, when bad men worship—and all men are bad: but he who would therefore abolish it abolishes his only hope of better men."[6] What is the statement getting at? Is it correct?

5. Several Protestant leaders who are in a position to know have said that the most effective evangelism today is being done by laymen. Does your experience confirm or deny this? What advantages does the lay evangelist have?

6. What is the relationship between stewardship and tithing?

7. Why, do you think, does Congress open its sessions with prayer?

CHAPTER 15

1. What is the difference between the words authoritative and authoritarian? Which best applies to the Sermon on the Mount?

2. A classical liturgical prayer begins, "O God, whose service is perfect freedom." Explain that phrase.

3. Why was the Sermon on the Mount preserved when most speeches from the same period were lost?

---

[4] *The Anatomy of Peace* by Emery Reves, p. 72. Copyright, 1945, by Emery Reves. Used by permission of Harper & Row, Publishers, Inc.

[5] *Christianity—and Our World* by John C. Bennett, p. 1. Association Press, 1936. Used by permission.

[6] *The Meaning of God in Human Experience* by William E. Hocking, p. 481. Yale University Press, 1912. Used by permission.

4. Do you agree with the quotation from Hunter? Base your answer on references to the biblical text of the Sermon.

5. One of the famous novels of the twentieth century is Arthur Koestler's *Darkness at Noon*. Ivanov, justifying the cruelty of a totalitarian government, says this:

"There are only two conceptions of human ethics, and they are at opposite poles. One of them is Christian and humane, declares the individual to be sacrosanct, and asserts that the rules of arithmetic are not to be applied to human units. The other starts from the basic principle that a collective aim justifies all means, and not only allows, but demands, that the individual should in every way be subordinated and sacrificed to the community—which may dispose of it as an experimental rabbit or a sacrificial lamb. . . . Do you know . . . a single example of a state which really follows a Christian policy? You can't point out one. In times of need—and politics are chronically times of need—the rulers were always able to evoke 'exceptional circumstances,' which demanded exceptional measures of defense."[7]

Is Ivanov right? Explain.

6. Thomas Jefferson said of slavery, "I tremble for my country when I reflect that God is just; that his justice cannot sleep forever." Compare this statement with Ivanov's.

---

[7] *Darkness at Noon* by Arthur Koestler, p. 157. The Macmillan Co., 1941. Used by permission.

In answer to Chapter 12, question 9, pages 109-110, General Marshall's word was *selflessness*.